Praise for *Constitution Translated for Kids:*

"Travis' book offer[s] ways to better understand the ideals and freedoms for which real patriots live—and die."

— Seattle Post Intelligencer

"*Constitution Translated for Kids* should be required reading for the September 11 generation."

— Momentum (National Catholic Educational Association)

"...make good use of local author Cathy Travis' ... *Constitution Translated for Kids* which offers the original text of the Constitution and Bill of Rights and a brisk, fifth-grade-level version in facing columns. Enlightenment for all."

— Washington Post

"*Constitution Translated For Kids* ... is a highly educational and informative presentation of what the language of the constitution really means ...."

— Midwest Book Review, 2003

"Ms. Travis did an excellent job in ... sticking to just the facts, ma'am."

— Bookloons

"You don't have to be a child to appreciate Travis' work. Travis ... gives us a version of the Constitution that we can all understand."

— Times Record News, Wichita Falls, TX

"It might prove useful for kids' parents, as well, because adults don't fare much better with their knowledge of the cornerstone document of American freedoms and protections."

— Austin American-Statesman

"Have you ever wondered why or what certain amendments mean? The title *Constitution Translated for Kids* says it all. This wonderfully written book takes what the constitution says and makes it easier to understand. Cathy Travis has done a superb job."

— Debra Gaynor for Reader Views

"Forget the schoolkids for a moment—every adult needs to take a few moments to read this book and get familiar with both the original document and the last two centuries of amendments to what was always intended to be a living document."

— Rambles, a cultural arts magazine

"In this carefully and thoughtfully written book the author answers ... many other questions.... [S]he begins by giving her readers a little background on the Founders and then goes on to explain what the Constitution is in the simplest of terms—a set of 'rules and directions.'"

— Through The Looking Glass Children's Book Review

"No other book ... gives an as easy-to-understand discussion of each sentence as this important document."

— School Library Journal

"I stand in total awe at the exceptional job author Cathy Travis has done in translating our Constitution into an uncomplicated way that anyone can read and understand. As I read this I smiled at finally having a full understanding of the document that governs my life and gives me my liberties. Well done; Bravo! I feel this book should be in every home in America; it is truly a God send for young and old alike."

— Midwest Book Review, 2005

W9-BVC-475

"This book should be in every library and home across the country—it is an excellent reference guide to the United States Constitution. The text is written in a fifth grade level, but is a perfectly suited for older readers as well."

— BookPleasures.com

"I wish this book had been published when I went to school! Cathy Travis is to be commended for making the Constitution comprehensible for young people. The addition of interesting facts, famous quotes and a glossary causes these pages to come alive with history and contemporary significance. Students, (as well as their parents!) will learn a lot more about this priceless document."

— *In the Library Reviews*

"It's hard to imagine a more important book ever being written for children. Cathy Travis' *Constitution Translated for Kids* is such a treasure. Not only does Travis succeed at explaining in detail the hows, whys and whats of the documents that this nation was founded upon, but she does so in a way that makes this information totally understandable and accessible, for kids as well as adults. A truly priceless book. No, I take that back. This book is a National Treasure."

— *Book Ideas*

"Travis includes exercises, proposed amendments and a glossary so the reader walks away with a solid grasp of the basic principles on which this nation was founded."

— *On the Bookshelf*

"This book does an excellent job of helping students understand the principles on which our country was founded."

— Rhode Island State Sen. Leo Blais

"This is a great opportunity to acquaint young students with the democratic process and to bring information about government and citizen participation into the classroom."

— Rhode Island Rep. House Deputy Minority
Whip Bruce J. Long

"When Cathy Travis puts her things together at the end of the day, there's one thing she never forgets: the Constitution."

— *Roll Call*

"Cathy Travis was pulling a little red wagon when she got started in politics.... Decades later, Travis is still talking, explaining and translating politics and government for the rest of us."

— *Scripps Howard News Service*

"Cathy Travis' first book, *Constitution Translated for Kids*, was almost 14 years in the making. Travis's book pairs the original text of the Constitution with an easy-to-read version targeted at fifth-graders."

— *The Hill*

Constitution

Translated

for Kids

FIFTH EDITION

CATHY TRAVIS

Constitution Translated for Kids

Constitution Translated for Kids may be purchased in bulk for educational use. For more information
or for a downloadable teacher's guide, please visit www.constitutionez.com.

http://www.travisbooks.com/constitution-for-kids/

This book is dedicated to
Sami, Rob, Tyler and Shelby
so you will have a clearer understanding
of the rights and responsibilities
of our democracy.

My deepest gratitude goes
to Cecilia,
who inspired me to undertake this endeavor;
to Mama Polly,
who inspires me always;
and to Mama,
who made it all possible.

Table of Contents

Foreword 13

Message to Teachers, Parents and Other Educators. 15

Message to Children 17

Birth of a Democracy 19

Article I (One) 21

Article II (Two) 31

Article III (Three) 35

Article IV (Four) 37

Article V (Five) 38

Article VI (Six) 39

Article VII (Seven) 40

The Bill of Rights (Amendments One (I) through Ten (X)) 42

Other Amendments (Eleven (XI) through Twenty-Seven (XXVII)) 46

Dividing It Up 60

Constitutional Compromises 62

Since the Constitution Was Written 63

Words to Look at While You Are Reading 65

Overview of the Constitution 69

Student Exercise in Democracy 90

Separating the Powers 99

Math of a Presidential Campaign 103

Bibliography 106

Foreword

The U.S. Constitution is the most revolutionary document ever produced by free people, and it set the stage for upheaval in the way nations all over the world governed the people they served. With the advent of the Constitution, for the first time people who were the "governed" were the ones who chose their leaders.

For us—today—that seems a rather bland, everyday occurrence. But when the Constitution was written and enacted, it was the death knell for kings and queens and other despots around the world. It ushered in an entirely new way of life for governing. It wasn't just that the Constitution put the fate of government in the hands of the masses, it was also the tremendous care the Framers (authors of the Constitution) took to make sure the states retained some manner of authority in the distribution of power.

It is the magical balance of power between the three co-equal branches of government under the Constitution (the Presidency, the Congress, and the Supreme Court) that ensures no one person—or small group of people—will ever have absolute power in this nation. This formula for government is what other nations modeled their own democracies upon in the nineteenth and twentieth centuries, and emerging democracies still do today.

This is the most important document ever written, and this book translating it for young people and families is one of the most important undertakings of our time. The nation is only as strong as its people, and the Constitution is only useful when our citizens use it. When people speak out, when reporters and observers write and broadcast as they please, when people of all faiths worship freely, when people gather together to pursue a common interest, when people petition their government, they exercise their rights and strengthen democracy in their country.

But when people do not know their rights, if they do not exercise them—like unused muscles—they weaken and go away. The Constitution protects us all: Republicans, Democrats, Independents—everyone in the United States.

That is why this is an exceptional book, for adults and children, for every American, and for anyone who has ever wondered how democracy is supposed to work.

State Representative Susan A. Story, Republican Co-Chair, Rhode Island Permanent Commission on Civic Education

State Senator Hanna M. Gallo, Democrat Co-Chair, Rhode Island Permanent Commission on Civic Education

Message to Teachers, Parents and Other Educators

Childhood years spent wondering how the government works, or what it is, while listening to TV news and hearing crotchety relatives disparage the government, begets apathetic adults. This book is an attempt to take what the Constitution says and make it easier to understand, so children will know their rights and protections under the Constitution. While no book can magically end political apathy, my hope is that this book will help teach kids what to expect from their government, its institutions and its leaders.

We are an electorate still very much moved by "force of personality." But it is the Constitution that endures, through each President and each Congress, the personalities of our leaders and the social dynamic of our times.

The foundation of all the laws in our country is the U.S. Constitution. It is our only common birthright as Americans. No other document supersedes the Constitution, yet precious few people understand this fact. The language of the times in which it was written, particularly the legalistic language of the late eighteenth century, makes the message of the Constitution awkward and sometimes difficult to understand.

For instance, most hunters know that the Second Amendment gives them the right to own a gun. But few know the original impetus of the amendment was to provide for a national guard. In 2009, the Supreme Court found an individual right to own a gun. Even fewer people know that the word "gun" does not actually appear in this amendment.

What usually surprises people the most about the Constitution is the discovery that by casting a vote for their candidate for President of the United States every four years in the general election, they essentially vote for electors (the results of the 2000 presidential election in Florida served as a fabulous civics' lesson on precisely this point).

The Constitution is ever-present in our lives. For example, when the nation was attacked in 2001, Congress (with the constitutional power to declare war) gave the President (the Commander-in-Chief of the armed forces of the United States) the authority to pursue the attackers militarily.

The text of the Constitution in this translation is gender-neutral . . . an interesting task, given that nearly all states ratifying the Constitution originally granted the right to vote only to white-male property owners over twenty-one. The very forward-thinking states (a small number) granted the right to vote to white males who did not own property. We have improved on our democracy since then.

This document created the most successful system of government known to people in the last two centuries, despite the human frailties of office holders and citizens. . . despite their emotions, doubts, fears, greed, anger, indecision, or bad decisions from time to time. The enduring magic of the Constitution is in the ideas this nation represents. Our independence was forged in the belief that our common pursuit of life, liberty and the pursuit of happiness would successfully govern a nation for the ages. The Constitution enshrines this philosophy.

There is no political message here, only the text of the Constitution presented in such a way that it can be easily understood. For those who doubt what the Constitution actually says, the original text of the Constitution, as written and adopted in 1787, appears on the left-hand side of the page (complete with Old English spelling and irregular caps), and the translation appears on the right-hand side of the page.

The only message in this book is that the ideas in the Constitution are relatively simple once people understand what they are. By no means is this a definitive work on the U.S. Constitution; there are plenty of other books offering in-depth studies of the Constitution, plus over two hundred years of Supreme Court decisions (which are the definitive word on constitutional issues). The purpose of this book is to make the essence of our Constitution easier to understand for young people.

At the back of this book is a glossary of terms, words that may be simple for adults but somewhat confusing for kids to understand. There is also context to guide adults in helping children retain what they are reading by answering questions, and engaging in exercises, that approximate some of the weighty decisions made in the name of our democracy.

Cathy Travis

Message to Children

*E*ver wonder what adults are talking about when they say things about the government? Or what it means when people say something is "constitutional?" Here's a way for you to set the adults straight.

When our country got started, there was a group of men called the "Founders." The Founders were people whose families came to this part of the world from Europe almost one hundred years before. They liked this place more than Europe, and they had a war to be independent.

They wanted to write down the rules and directions for a new and fair government, so they wrote the Constitution. These rules that they wrote down have been our guidelines (directions) for how to run the country for over two centuries. Just like we have rules for football, basketball or soccer, we have rules for running the government.

You may wonder what the rules are that everybody always seems to talk about and where they can be found. These are our rules, all in the U.S. Constitution. It has seven parts called Articles, some longer and harder to understand than others, plus twenty-seven additions called Amendments. Some of these amendments are also long and hard to understand.

On the left-hand side of the page are the actual words of the U.S. Constitution from 1787, so if somebody doesn't believe you, you can show them the words used in the real thing. There may still be some hard words in the translation on the right-hand side; they are listed in the back to tell you what they mean.

This is a wonderful country, and it is important for everyone to know what the rules are. If more people know these rules, our country will be a better place. And, the more people understand these rules, the more likely they are to participate in our government. If you know your rights, the Constitution will always work for you.

Help teach the adults what the Constitution actually says.

Cathy Travis

Birth of a Democracy

Timeline Leading to a Constitutional Government
in the United States

Throughout the 1700s, the British ruler, King George III, demanded a lot of the North American colonists: collecting huge taxes, insisting British soldiers stay in colonists' homes, and allowing soldiers to be cruel and abusive to the people.

The last half of the century would divide American colonies further and further from the British, setting the stage for the Revolutionary War for independence and a new government for a nation that would become the United States of America, governed by the Constitution.

1770 — At the "Boston Massacre" five American civilians were killed by British troops, an event that helped spark the American Revolutionary War.

1773 — The Boston Tea Party was a protest by the American colonists against Great Britain during which they destroyed many crates of tea bricks on ships in Boston Harbor. The incident accelerated the march to a revolution.

1773–1774 — King George's British Parliament passed a series of abusive and insulting laws in response to the Boston Tea Party. King George and the British government hoped that, by making an example of Boston, these spiteful measures would stop the colonies from wanting independence. American colonists called the series of laws "The Intolerable Acts." The acts caused anger and conflict in the colonies and were important in the spread of the American Revolution.

1774 — Several states wanted a congress of all the colonies to resist King George. The colonies named delegates to the First Continental Congress. The First Continental Congress met briefly and then set up its successor, the Second Continental Congress, which would meet two years later and organize the American colonies into war against Britain.

1775 — The first battle of the American Revolution was at Lexington and Concord, near Boston. The battle began the open war between King George/Britain and its thirteen colonies in North America.

1775 — The Battle of Bunker Hill was a vicious battle eventually won by the British, who suffered more than 1,000 casualties. But it showed the British the Americans were ready for the war.

1776 — The Second Continental Congress met in Philadelphia. John Hancock was elected president of the Congress, and George Washington was named commander-in-chief of the Continental Army. The Continental Congress met until 1781. During the Revolutionary War, it acted as the U.S. national government by raising armies, picking diplomats, and making treaties with other countries.

1776 — On July 2, the Continental Congress voted in favor of independence; on July 4, the Declaration of Independence was approved. Copies were sent throughout the colonies to be read publicly.

1776–1783 — The bloody and devastating revolutionary war for American independence lasted seven years.

1777 — The Continental Congress passed the Articles of Confederation, which gave power largely to the states, making a national government unworkable.

1783 — The Continental Congress declared the war with England over on April 15. The Treaty of Paris of 1783, signed on September 3, 1783, formally ended the American Revolutionary War.

1783–1787 — The young nation struggled to operate under the Articles of Confederation. They realized they cannot, so they convene a constitutional convention to come up with a new form of government.

1787 — September 17, the Continental Congress adopted the Constitution of the United States.

1787 — September 28, the Constitution went to the states for approval.

1787 — The states of Delaware, Pennsylvania and New Jersey ratified the Constitution.

1788 — The states of Georgia, Connecticut, Massachusetts, Maryland, South Carolina, Virginia and New York ratified the Constitution.

1788 — On June 21, New Hampshire became the ninth state to ratify the new Constitution, making its adoption official.

1788 — On July 2, the Continental Congress stepped aside for the new government. The U.S. Constitution began governing.

1789 — The first Congress of the United States was sworn in, as directed by Article I of the Constitution.

1789 — George Washington became the young nation's first President in accordance with Article II of the Constitution.

Fast Fact

The U.S. Constitution is the shortest, and the oldest, Constitution of any government in the world.

Complete Text of the United States Constitution (1789)	Translation of the Complete Text of the United States Constitution

We the People of the United States, in Order to form a more perfect Union, establish Justice, insure domestic Tranquility, provide for the common defence, promote the general Welfare, and secure the Blessings of Liberty to ourselves and our Posterity, do ordain and establish this Constitution for the United States of America.

We the People of the United States—so we can make a country, get along fairly, stay safe, defend ourselves, take care of each other and make sure we and our children stay free— join together to write the highest, most supreme law of the United States in this Constitution.

ARTICLE I

SECTION 1. All legislative Powers herein granted shall be vested in a Congress of the United States, which shall consist of a Senate and House of Representatives.

SECTION 2. The House of Representatives shall be composed of Members chosen every second Year by the People of the several States, and the Electors in each State shall have the Qualifications requisite for Electors of the most numerous Branch of the State Legislature.

No Person shall be a Representative who shall not have attained to the Age of twenty five Years, and been seven Years a Citizen of the United States, and who shall not, when elected, be an Inhabitant of that State in which he shall be chosen.

ARTICLE I

SECTION 1. Laws are made by Congress. Congress is made up of a Senate and a House of Representatives.

SECTION 2. Members of the House of Representatives are elected every two years. The people who are registered to vote are the same people who get to vote for members of the biggest house of the state legislature.

To get elected to the House, you must be twenty-five years old, be a citizen of the United States for at least seven years, and live in the same state that elects you.

Representatives and direct Taxes shall be apportioned among the several States which may be included within this Union, according to their respective Numbers, which shall be determined by adding to the whole Number of free Persons, including those bound to Service for a Term of Years, and excluding Indians not taxed, three fifths of all other Persons. The actual Enumeration shall be made within three Years after the first Meeting of the Congress of the United States, and within every subsequent Term of ten Years, in such Manner as they shall by Law direct. The number of Representatives shall not exceed one for every thirty Thousand, but each State shall have at Least one Representative; and until such enumeration shall be made, the State of New Hampshire shall be entitled to chuse three, Massachusetts eight, Rhode-Island and Providence Plantations one, Connecticut five, New-York six, New Jersey, four, Pennsylvania eight, Delaware one, Maryland six, Virginia ten, North Carolina five, South Carolina five, and Georgia three.

(Representatives and taxes were originally based on population; slaves and Indians did not count as full people. Section 2 of the Fourteenth Amendment changed how people are counted.)

Representatives in Congress, as well as taxes (this part about taxes was changed by the Sixteenth Amendment), are spread out over the country and are based on the number of people living in the places they represent.

People in the country are counted every ten years in a census, so we know how many people live in the United States. The census also helps us figure out how many people are represented in the House of Representatives and helps the government determine taxes. A certain number of people (originally thirty thousand; now over five-hundred thousand) have their own representative.

For the first Congress, with no census, the division of representatives in the House was: New Hampshire, three; Massachusetts, eight; Rhode Island and Providence Plantations, one; Connecticut, five; New York, six; New Jersey, four; Pennsylvania, eight; Delaware, one; Maryland, six; Virginia, ten; North Carolina, five; South Carolina, five; and Georgia, three.

When vacancies happen in the Representation from any State, the Executive Authority thereof shall issue Writs of Election to fill such Vacancies.

If a representative leaves office or dies, the governor of that state sets up another election and a new representative is elected.

The House of Representatives shall chuse their Speaker and other Officers; and shall have the sole Power of Impeachment.

Representatives pick a Speaker and other officers to run the House of Representatives. Only the House of Representatives can vote to start the process for kicking somebody out of office (impeaching them).

SECTION 3. The Senate of the United States shall be composed of two Senators from each State, chosen by the Legislature thereof, for six Years; and each Senator shall have one Vote.

Immediately after they shall be assembled in Consequence of the first Election, they shall be divided as equally as may be into three Classes. The Seats of the Senators of the first Class shall be vacated at the Expiration of the second Year, of the second Class at the Expiration of the fourth Year, and of the third Class at the Expiration of the sixth Year, so that one third may be chosen every second Year; and if Vacancies happen by Resignation, or otherwise, during the Recess of the Legislature of any State, the Executive thereof may make temporary Appointments until the next Meeting of the Legislature, which shall then fill such Vacancies.

No Person shall be a Senator who shall not have attained to the Age of thirty Years, and been nine Years a Citizen of the United States, and who shall not, when elected, be an Inhabitant of that State for which he shall be chosen.

The Vice President of the United States shall be President of the Senate, but shall have no Vote, unless they be equally divided.

The Senate shall chuse their other Officers, and also a President pro tempore, in the Absence of the Vice President, or when he shall exercise the Office of President of the United States.

The Senate shall have sole Power to try all Impeachments. When sitting for that Purpose, they shall be on Oath or Affirma-

SECTION 3. Originally, senators were chosen by the state legislatures, but the Seventeenth Amendment changed that, so the people in the states could vote directly for their senators.

The United States Senate has two senators from each state, elected every six years. Each senator has one vote in the Senate.

After the first election of senators in the U.S., they will divide themselves into three groups, each picking a term of two, four or six years for their first term so after that, one-third of the senators are elected every two years.

If a senator leaves office or dies in the middle of his or her term of office, the governor of that state can pick someone to temporarily be the senator until the next election is held.

To be a senator, you have to be thirty years old, be a citizen of the United States for at least nine years and live in the state that elects you.

The Vice President of the United States is the President of the Senate, but only gets to vote if there is a tie (the number of "yes" votes and the number of "no" votes are the same).

The Senate gets to pick another President of the Senate for the times when the Vice President cannot be there.

The Senate holds the trials for people the House of Representatives thinks should be impeached. If the Senate is trying to

tion. When the President of the United States is tried, the Chief Justice shall preside: And no Person shall be convicted without the Concurrence of two thirds of the Members present.

Judgement in Cases of Impeachment shall not extend further than to removal from Office, and disqualification to hold and enjoy any Office of honor, Trust or Profit under the United States; but the Party convicted shall nevertheless be liable and subject to Indictment, Trial, Judgement and Punishment, according to Law.

SECTION 4. The Times, Places and Manner of holding Elections for Senators and Representatives, shall be prescribed in each State by the Legislature thereof; but the Congress may at any time by Law make or alter such Regulations, except as to the Places of chusing Senators.

The Congress shall assemble at least once in every Year, and such Meeting shall be on the first Monday in December, unless they shall by Law appoint a different Day.

SECTION 5. Each House shall be the Judge of the Elections, Returns and Qualifications of its own Members, and a Majority of each shall constitute a Quorum to do Business; but a smaller Number may adjourn from day to day, and may be authorized to compel the Attendance of absent Members, in such manner, and under such Penalties as each House may provide.

impeach someone (kick them out of office), everyone has to swear to tell the truth. If the President of the United States is being tried, the Chief Justice of the United States is in charge of the trial. But no one can get kicked out of office unless two-thirds of the senators present at the trial vote to kick them out.

Anyone impeached by Congress cannot be re-elected or appointed to another office. If someone is impeached, and then gets kicked out of office, that person can still be tried before a criminal or civil jury for any crimes committed, just like the law says.

SECTION 4. The state legislature picks the times and places for elections, but Congress can make laws to change the election times and places for senators and representatives. Originally, Congress could not change the rules about where senators were chosen, but the Seventeenth Amendment changed that.

The Congress will meet at least once every year, at a regular time unless they make a new law to change it to another day (originally, they were to meet on the first Monday in December, but Section 2 of the Twentieth Amendment changed that to noon on January 3).

SECTION 5. The House of Representatives and the Senate are each in charge of the elections and behavior of their members. Both the House of Representatives and the Senate need most of their members present in order to do business. They can make their members come to work, and if they do not come, they can punish them.

Each House may determine the Rules of its Proceedings, punish its Members for disorderly Behaviour, and, with the Concurrence of two thirds, expel a Member.

Both the House of Representatives and the Senate make their own rules for doing business. They can punish members for misbehaving, and they can kick members out if two-thirds of them vote for it.

Each House shall keep a Journal of its Proceedings, and from time to time publish the same, excepting such Parts as may in their Judgment require Secrecy; and the Yeas and Nays of the Members of either House on any question shall, at the Desire of one fifth of those Present, be entered on the Journal.

Both the House of Representatives and the Senate write down what they say and do in a journal and print it so everybody can read it, unless it is really secret. Votes of individual representatives or senators must be written down if twenty percent of the members want that.

Neither House, during the Session of Congress, shall, without the Consent of the other, adjourn for more than three days, nor to any other Place than that in which the two Houses shall be sitting.

While Congress is meeting, the House of Representatives or the Senate cannot leave for more than three days, unless they both decide to leave.

SECTION 6. The Senators and Representatives shall receive a Compensation for their Services, to be ascertained by Law, and paid out of the Treasury of the United States. They shall in all Cases, except Treason, Felony and Breach of the Peace, be privileged from Arrest during their Attendance at the Session of their respective Houses, and in going to and returning from the same; and for any Speech or Debate in either House, they shall not be questioned in any other Place.

SECTION 6. Senators and representatives will get paid by the government according to the law. Except for treason, stealing, or disturbing the peace, they cannot be arrested while they are at work, or on their way to work, in Congress.

Congress modified this a little bit in the Twenty-Seventh Amendment, making any change in pay for Congress apply to the next Congress, not the one that voted for it.

No Senator or Representative shall, during the Time for which he was elected, be appointed to any civil Office under the Authority of the United States, which shall have been created, or the Emoluments whereof shall have been encreased during such time; and no Person holding any Office under the United States, shall be a Member of either House during his Continuance in Office.

No senator or representative can be picked for another office in the U.S. government if that office was created, or if the office got a pay raise, while that senator or representative was in Congress. No one can serve in Congress and work somewhere else in the government at the same time.

SECTION 7. All Bills for raising Revenue shall originate in the House of Representatives; but the Senate may propose or concur with amendments as on other Bills.

Every Bill which shall have passed the House of Representatives and the Senate, shall, before it becomes a Law, be presented to the President of the United States; If he approve he shall sign it, but if not he shall return it, with his Objections to that House in which it shall have originated, who shall enter the Objections at large on their Journal, and proceed to reconsider it. If after such Reconsideration two thirds of that House shall agree to pass the Bill, it shall be sent, together with the Objections, to the other House, by which it shall likewise be reconsidered, and if approved by two thirds of that House, it shall become a Law. But in all such Cases the Votes of both Houses shall be determined by yeas and Nays, and the Names of the Persons voting for and against the Bill shall be entered on the Journal of each House respectively. If any Bill shall not be returned by the President within ten Days (Sundays excepted) after it shall have been presented to him, the Same shall be a law, in like Manner as if he had signed it, unless the Congress by their Adjournment prevent its Return, in which Case it shall not be a law.

Every Order, Resolution, or Vote to which the Concurrence of the Senate and House of Representatives may be necessary (except on a question of Adjournment) shall be presented to the President of the United States; and before the Same shall take Effect, shall be approved by him, or being

SECTION 7. Any bill raising money (taxes) must begin in the House of Representatives, but the Senate must agree with it, just like any other bill.

When a bill passes both the House and the Senate, the bill goes to the President who must sign it to make it the law. If the President agrees with the bill, he or she signs it—but if the President does not agree with the bill within ten days, he or she writes down why and sends that letter and the bill back to the House of Representatives or the Senate, wherever the bill got started. When Congress gets the letter and the bill back from the President, the House of Representatives or the Senate puts it all in their journal. Then they talk about it some more and vote on it again. If two-thirds of the representatives and senators vote for the same bill again, it becomes law. The representatives and the senators must have their votes written down in their journal. If the President does not sign the bill, or does not send the bill back to Congress in ten days (not counting Sunday), then it becomes law, unless Congress officially leaves to go home (adjourns).

Each law passed by the House of Representatives and the Senate must be signed by the President. The laws the President does not agree with (those that get "vetoed") must be passed by two-thirds of the House of Representatives and the Senate before they can become law.

disapproved by him, shall be repassed by two thirds of the Senate and House of Representatives, according to the Rules and Limitations prescribed in the Case of a Bill.

SECTION 8. The Congress shall have Power To lay and collect Taxes, Duties, Imposts and Excises, to pay the Debts and provide for the common Defence and general Welfare of the United States; but all Duties, Imposts and Excises shall be uniform throughout the United States;

SECTION 8. Congress has the job of raising and spending money to take care of the nation, but all taxes raised must be the same for all the states. Here are some of the other jobs Congress performs:

To borrow Money on the credit of the United States;

To borrow money using the credit of the United States.

To regulate Commerce with foreign Nations, and among the several States, and with the Indian Tribes;

To make rules for how people do business, including buying and selling things with people in other countries, among the states and with Native Americans.

To establish a uniform Rule of Naturalization, and uniform Laws on the subject of Bankruptcies throughout the United States;

To decide on fair rules for letting people become citizens—and rules for bankruptcies in all the states.

To coin Money, regulate the Value thereof, and of foreign Coin, and fix the Standard of Weights and Measures;

To print paper money and make coins, and figure out how much it will be worth, and how much the money from other countries will be worth, and decide on a system of weights and measures.

To provide for the Punishment of counterfeiting the Securities and current Coin of the United States;

To punish people who copy money or bonds of the United States.

To establish Post Offices and post Roads;

To build post offices and roads.

To promote the Progress of Science and useful Arts, by securing for limited Times to Authors and Inventors the exclusive Right to their respective Writings and Discoveries;

To promote science and the arts by giving copyrights to writers and inventors for things they write and discover.

To constitute Tribunals inferior to the supreme Court;

To keep a system of courts around the country to support the Supreme Court.

To define and punish Piracies and Felonies committed on the high Seas, and Offenses against the Law of Nations;

To make laws about what people can and cannot do on the oceans.

To declare War, grant Letters of Marque and Reprisal, and make Rules concerning Captures on Land and Water;

To make war, allow private boats and vessels to catch and arrest enemy ships, and make rules about taking prisoners on the land and on the water.

To raise and support Armies, but no Appropriation of money to that Use shall be for a longer Term than two Years;

To build an army and pay for it—but money for the army can only be given for, at the most, two years at a time.

To provide and maintain a Navy;

To build a navy and pay for it.

To make Rules for the Government and Regulation of the land and naval Forces;

To make all the rules for the government and the army and the navy.

To provide for calling forth the Militia to execute the Laws of the Union, suppress Insurrections and repel Invasions;

To make rules for calling the states' National Guards to force people to obey the law, stop riots and to fight attackers.

To provide for organizing, arming, and disciplining, the Militia, and for governing such Part of them as may be employed in the Service of the United States, reserving to the States respectively, the Appointment of the Officers, and the Authority of training the Militia according to the discipline prescribed by Congress;

To organize the states' National Guards and give them guns and equipment and be in charge of them if they are working for the United States. But the states get to be in charge of the training Congress wants, and the states each get to pick the officers of the National Guard in their state.

To exercise exclusive Legislation in all Cases whatsoever, over such District (not exceeding ten Miles square) as may, by Cession of particular States, and the Acceptance of Congress, become the Seat of the Government of the United States, and to exercise like Authority over all Places purchased by the Consent of the Legislature of the State in which the Same shall be, for the Erection of Forts, Magazines, Arsenals, dock-Yards, and other needful Buildings;—And

To be in charge of a place, no bigger than ten square miles, a place given by the states and accepted by Congress that will be the seat of the federal government. (This is present-day Washington, D.C.) Congress will be in charge of all the places bought and run by the government, —AND—

To make all Laws which shall be necessary and proper for carrying into Execution the foregoing Powers, and all other Powers vested by this Constitution in the Government of the United States, or in any Department or Officer thereof.

SECTION 9. The Migration or Importation of such Persons as any of the States now existing shall think proper to admit, shall not be prohibited by the Congress prior to the Year one thousand eight hundred and eight, but a Tax or duty may be imposed on such Importation, not exceeding ten dollars for each Person.

The Privilege of the Writ of Habeas Corpus shall not be suspended, unless when in Cases of Rebellion or Invasion the public Safety may require it.

No Bill of Attainder or ex post facto Law shall be passed.

No Capitation, or other direct, Tax shall be laid, unless in Proportion to the Census or Enumeration herein before directed to be taken.

No Tax or Duty shall be laid on Articles exported from any State.

No Preference shall be given by any Regulation of Commerce or Revenue to the Ports of one State over those of another: nor shall Vessels bound to, or from, one

To make all the laws Congress needs to enforce the powers given to it by this Constitution.

SECTION 9. Congress cannot ban the international slave trade until at least 1808, but a tax of up to ten dollars can be put on imported slaves.

(Slavery was banned by the Thirteenth Amendment.)

People who are arrested and put in jail have the right to make the government tell them why they were put in jail. This right can be taken away only if there is a rebellion, or if the United States is invaded by a foreign power.

Congress cannot pass a law declaring someone guilty of a crime. Criminal laws passed by Congress can only be applied to crimes that are committed after the law is passed.

Congress must tax according to the number of citizens there are in the country based on the census.

(The Sixteenth Amendment changed this so Congress could charge and collect taxes any way they wanted.)

Congress cannot tax things sold from one state to another state.

Congress cannot show preference for one port over another port, and no ship from one state can get taxed for using another state's port.

State, be obliged to enter, clear, or pay Duties in another.

No Money shall be drawn from the Treasury, but in Consequence of Appropriations made by Law; and a regular Statement and Account of the Receipts and Expenditures of all public Money shall be published from time to time.

No money can be spent without Congress passing a law for it, and they should publish a regular statement of the Treasury account from time to time.

No Title of Nobility shall be granted by the United States: And no Person holding any Office of Profit or Trust under them, shall, without the Consent of the Congress, accept of any present, Emolument, Office, or Title, of any kind whatever, from any King, Prince, or foreign State.

Congress cannot give anyone a title of nobility (king, queen, prince, lord, etc.); and, no officer of the United States can accept any title, office or payment of any kind from any other country.

SECTION 10. No State shall enter into any Treaty, Alliance, or Confederation; grant Letters of Marque and Reprisal; coin Money; emit Bills of Credit; make any Thing but gold and silver Coin a Tender in Payment of Debts; pass any Bill of Attainder, ex post facto Law, or Law impairing the Obligation of Contracts, or grant any Title of Nobility.

SECTION 10. No state can ally (become a partner) with another country; make war; make their own money; allow private boats and vessels to catch and arrest enemy ships; or issue their own bills for credit. States can make only silver and gold to pay for things. States cannot pass any law to disgrace people accused of dishonor. States cannot pass a law that goes back in time. Laws can be applied only after they are passed. States cannot pass a law that messes up contracts already in force. States may not give people a title of nobility.

No State shall, without the Consent of the Congress, lay any Imposts or duties on Imports or Exports, except what may be absolutely necessary for executing it's inspection Laws: and the net Produce of all Duties and Imposts, laid by any State on Imports or Exports, shall be for the Use of the Treasury of the United States; and all such Laws shall be subject to the Revision and Controul of the Congress.

States must have the permission of Congress to charge money for buying and selling things that come into the country and things sold outside of the country. If states pass laws to charge money for things that come into and go out of the country, all the money collected will go to the United States Treasury. Congress can make laws to change or control these state laws.

No State shall, without the Consent of Congress, lay any Duty of Tonnage, keep Troops, or Ships of War in time of Peace, enter into any Agreement or Compact with another State, or with a foreign Power, or engage in War, unless actually invaded, or in such imminent Danger as will not admit of delay.

States must have Congress' permission to keep armies or warships during peacetime. States will need Congress' permission to join forces with another state, or with a foreign power, or to make war, unless they are invaded and the United States' troops cannot get there in time to help them.

ARTICLE II

SECTION 1. The executive Power shall be vested in a President of the United States of America. He shall hold his Office during the Term of four Years, and, together with the Vice President, chosen for the same Term, be elected, as follows:

Each State shall appoint, in such Manner as the Legislature thereof may direct, a Number of Electors, equal to the whole Number of Senators and Representatives to which the State may be entitled in the Congress: but no Senator or Representative, or Person holding an Office of Trust or Profit under the United States, shall be appointed an Elector.

The Electors shall meet in their respective States, and vote by Ballot for two Persons, of whom one at least shall not be an Inhabitant of the same State with themselves. And they shall make a List of all the Persons voted for, and of the Number of Votes for each; which List they shall sign and certify, and transmit sealed to the Seat of the Government of the United States, directed to the President of the Senate.

ARTICLE II

SECTION 1. The leader of the country will be the President of the United States. The President will be elected every four years, along with a Vice President, like this:

The legislature of each state decides how that state will name a number of people called "electors." The number of electors will equal the number of representatives and senators of that state—senators, representatives, or other government officers cannot be electors. (If a state has four representatives and two senators, it has six electors who are members of what is now known as the Electoral College.)

The electors meet in their states and vote for two people. At least one person for whom they vote cannot live in that elector's state. The electors make a list of all the people they voted for and how many votes each person got. Then, they sign and certify the list and send it to the President of the Senate in the seat of the United States government (Washington, D.C.). The President of the Senate opens all the

The President of the Senate shall, in the Presence of the Senate and House of Representatives, open all the Certificates, and the Votes shall then be counted. The Person having the greatest Number of Votes shall be the President, if such Number be a Majority of the whole Number of Electors appointed; and if there be more than one who have such Majority, and have an equal Number of Votes, then the House of Representatives shall immediately chuse by Ballot one of them for President; and if no Person have a majority, then from the five highest on the List the said House shall in like Manner chuse the President. But in chusing the President, the Votes shall be taken by States, the Representation from each State having one Vote; A quorum for this Purpose shall consist of a Member or Members from two-thirds of the States, and a Majority of all the States shall be necessary to a Choice. In every Case, after the Choice of the President, the Person having the greatest Number of Votes of the Electors shall be the Vice President. But if there should remain two or more who have equal Votes, the Senate shall chuse from them by Ballot the Vice President.

The Congress may determine the Time of chusing the Electors, and the Day on which they shall give their Votes; which Day shall be the same throughout the United States.

No Person except a natural born Citizen, or a Citizen of the United States, at the time of the Adoption of this Constitution, shall be eligible to the Office of President; neither shall any person be eligible to that Office who shall not have attained to the Age of thirty-five Years, and been fourteen Years a Resident within the United States.

states' certificates in front of the representatives and senators, and then the votes are counted. The person with the majority of electors' votes will be the President of the United States. If more than one person has the same number of electors' votes, the representatives will immediately choose one of the people by a vote. If nobody has a majority, then the representatives will choose a President from among the five people who got the most electors' votes. But if the representatives have to choose a President like this, the vote will be taken by states and each state has only one vote. At least two-thirds of the representatives must be present to choose a President in this way. If the President has to be chosen like this, the person with the next highest number of electors' votes will be the Vice President. If there is a tie, the senators vote for the Vice President.

(The Twelfth Amendment and the Twenty-Third Amendment changed this process.)

Congress picks the time for choosing electors, and the day they will vote. It will be the same day in all states.

The President must be born in the United States (or to U.S. citizens), be thirty-five years old, and have lived in the United States for at least fourteen years.

32

In Case of the Removal of the President from Office, or of his Death, Resignation, or Inability to discharge the Powers and Duties of the said Office, the Same shall devolve on the Vice President, and the Congress may by Law provide for the Case of Removal, Death, Resignation or Inability, both of the President and Vice President, declaring what Officer shall then act as President, and such Officer shall act accordingly, until the Disability be removed, or a President shall be elected.

If the President dies, leaves office, is kicked out, or is unable to do the job, the duties of President fall to the Vice President. If the Vice President dies, leaves office, gets kicked out, or is unable to do the job, then Congress figures out which officer will act as President if the elected President or Vice President is unable to do his or her job. Whoever is chosen to be President or Vice President will hold that office until the elected President or Vice President can do his or her job again, or until another Presidential election is held and a new President or Vice President is elected. (This got more specific with the Twenty-Fifth Amendment.)

The President shall, at stated Times, receive for his Services, a Compensation, which shall neither be increased nor diminished during the Period for which he shall have been elected, and he shall not receive within that period any other Emolument from the United States, or any of them.

The President will get paid for serving as President, and his or her pay cannot go up or down while he or she serves as President. The President cannot get paid anything but a salary from the United States while President. The President cannot get money from any state.

Before he enter on the Execution of his Office, he shall take the following Oath or Affirmation: "I do solemnly swear (or affirm) that I will faithfully execute the Office of President of the United States, and will to the best of my Ability, preserve, protect and defend the Constitution of the United States."

When the President takes office, this is the oath he or she will take: "I do solemnly swear (or affirm) that I will faithfully execute the Office of President of the United States, and will to the best of my ability, preserve, protect and defend the Constitution of the United States."

SECTION 2. The President shall be the Commander in Chief of the Army and Navy of the United States, and of the Militia of the several States, when called into the actual service of the United States; he may require the Opinion, in writing, of the principal Officer in each of the executive Departments, upon any

SECTION 2. The President is the Commander-in-Chief in charge of the army, navy and all the armed forces of the United States. The President is also in charge of the National Guard of the states when the National Guard is working for the United States. The President may get the officers of the executive departments to write

Subject relating to the Duties of their respective Offices, and he shall have Power to grant Reprieves and Pardons for Offenses against the United States, except in Cases of Impeachment.

He shall have Power, by and with the Advice and Consent of the Senate, to make Treaties, provided two-thirds of the Senators present concur; and he shall nominate, and by and with the Advice and Consent of the Senate, shall appoint Ambassadors, other public Ministers and Consuls, Judges of the supreme Court, and all other Officers of the United States, whose Appointments are not herein otherwise provided for, and which shall be established by Law: but the Congress may by Law vest the Appointment of such inferior Officers, as they think proper, in the President alone, in the Courts of Law, or in the Heads of Departments.

The President shall have Power to fill up all Vacancies that may happen during the Recess of the Senate, by granting Commissions which shall expire at the End of their next Session.

SECTION 3. He shall from time to time give to the Congress Information of the State of the Union, and recommend to their Consideration such Measures as he shall judge necessary and expedient; he may, on extraordinary Occasions, convene both Houses, or either of them, and in Case of Disagreement between them, with Respect to the Time of Adjournment, he may adjourn them to such Time as he

down their ideas about anything they are in charge of. The President can pardon people for crimes against the United States, except when those people get impeached by the House of Representatives and found guilty by the Senate.

The President has the power to make treaties, with the advice and permission of two-thirds of the senators present. The President can also appoint, with the direction and permission of two-thirds of the senators, ambassadors (U.S. representatives in other countries), Supreme Court judges and other U.S. officers. Congress must approve the President's appointments in these matters with a two-thirds vote of senators present. Congress will decide how other appointments will be handled. Congress can let the President, the courts, or department heads appoint other officers as they see fit.

If Congress is not in session, the President can fill vacancies for positions whose terms end at the end of the next session of Congress.

SECTION 3. The President tells Congress how the country is doing in a "State of the Union" speech from time to time. The President also gives Congress ideas about how to get things done; and the President can meet with Congress anytime he or she thinks it is really important. If the Congress cannot agree on some of the issues before them when they are finished working for the year, the President can dismiss

Fast Fact
The Constitutional Convention adjourned at four o'clock in the afternoon.

shall think proper; he shall receive Ambassadors and other public Ministers; he shall take Care that the Laws be faithfully executed, and shall Commission all the Officers of the United States.

the Congress and then call them back into session at a time he or she thinks is fair. The President welcomes ambassadors or government representatives from other countries. The President is also in charge of making sure that the laws are carried out fairly; and, the President gives authority and legal power to all the officers of the United States.

SECTION 4. The President, Vice President and all civil Officers of the United States, shall be removed from Office on Impeachment for, and Conviction of, Treason, Bribery, or other high Crimes and Misdemeanors.

SECTION 4. The President, the Vice President and other officers of the United States, can be kicked out of office (impeached) if they are found guilty of double-crossing (betraying) the country, offering people money, or getting money to do something dishonest, or any other really big crimes.

ARTICLE III

SECTION 1. The judicial Power of the United States, shall be vested in one supreme Court, and in such inferior Courts as the Congress may from time to time ordain and establish. The Judges, both of the supreme and inferior Courts, shall hold their Offices during good Behaviour, and shall, at stated Times, receive for their Services, a Compensation, which shall not be diminished during their Continuance in Office.

SECTION 2. The judicial Power shall extend to all Cases, in Law and Equity, arising under this Constitution, the Laws

ARTICLE III

SECTION 1. All the judicial power of the United States, including the courts of law and justice, will be headed by one Supreme Court. Congress can set up other courts when we need them. The judges on the Supreme Court, and the other courts under them, can stay judges all their lives if they obey all the laws. The salary judges get paid for their service cannot be lowered during their time as a judge.

SECTION 2. The judges of the courts have the power to decide any case that involves or questions the Constitution, the laws of of the United States, and Treaties made, or which shall be made, under their Authority;—to all Cases affecting Ambassadors, other public Ministers and Consuls;—to all Cases of admiralty and maritime Jurisdiction;—to Controversies to which the United States shall be a Party;—to Controversies between two or more States;— between a State and Citizens of another State; —between Citizens of different States— between Citizens of the same State claiming Lands under Grants of different States, and between a State, or the Citizens thereof, and foreign States, Citizens or Subjects.

the United States, or any treaty signed by the United States. The courts also decide cases that involve ambassadors or foreign ministers from other countries. The courts have the final say on cases that involve actions that take place on the oceans. They decide arguments that involve the United States, disputes between two or more states, or between a state and somebody from another country, cases between citizens of different states, or between citizens of the same state when different states give them the same land, and to all cases between a state, the citizens in that state and other countries and their citizens.

(This was all changed by the Eleventh Amendment.)

In all Cases affecting Ambassadors, other public Ministers and Consuls, and those in which a State shall be Party, the supreme Court shall have original Jurisdiction. In all the other Cases before mentioned, the supreme Court shall have appellate Jurisdiction, both as to Law and Fact, with such Exceptions, and under such Regulations as the Congress shall make.

If an ambassador or minister from another country, or if a state is involved, the Supreme Court can hear the case first. In all the other cases, the smaller courts will hear the cases first, and the losers can then appeal their case. The Supreme Court is the final authority. It can look at both the law and the facts of each case with the rules Congress has passed.

The Trial of all Crimes, except in Cases of Impeachment; shall be by Jury; and such Trial shall be held in the State where the said Crimes shall have been committed; but when not committed within any State, the Trial shall be at such Place or Places as the Congress may by Law have directed.

Trial for all federal crimes, except kicking people out of government (impeaching them), will be in front of a jury. The trial will be held in the same state where the crime is committed. If the crime is not committed in a state (like on the ocean), Congress can decide by law where to hold the trial.

SECTION 3. Treason against the United States, shall consist only in levying War against them, or in adhering to their Enemies, giving them Aid and Comfort. No Person shall be convicted of Treason

SECTION 3. Treason, or betraying the United States, is considered making war against the United States, or being loyal to an enemy of the United States, or giving that enemy help or comfort. Nobody can be

unless on the Testimony of two Witnesses to the same overt Act, or on Confession in open Court.

The Congress shall have Power to declare the Punishment of Treason, but no Attainder of Treason shall work Corruption of Blood, or Forfeiture except during the Life of the Person attainted.

found guilty of treason unless two people describe the same obvious act of treason in open court, or unless the accused person says in open court that he or she did it.

Congress decides how to punish treason. If someone is guilty of treason, his or her family cannot be punished for the crimes that person commits. The disgrace of the traitor, and any fines he or she may owe, goes with him or her to their death, but not past that.

ARTICLE IV

SECTION 1. Full Faith and Credit shall be given in each State to the public Acts, Records, and judicial Proceedings of every other State; And the Congress may by general Laws prescribe the Manner in which such Acts, Records and Proceedings shall be proved and the Effect thereof.

SECTION 2. The Citizens of each State shall be entitled to all Privileges and Immunities of Citizens in the several States.

A Person charged in any State with Treason, Felony, or other Crime, who shall flee from Justice, and be found in another State, shall on Demand of the executive Authority of the State from which he fled, be delivered up, to be removed to the State having Jurisdiction of the Crime.

No Person held to Service or Labour in one State, under the Laws thereof, escaping into another, shall, in Consequence of any

ARTICLE IV

SECTION 1. Each state will honor every other state's public acts, their records and their legal reports. The Congress will make laws to decide how to check on such acts, records and reports. Congress will decide how to test these records and how effective they are.

SECTION 2. Citizens of each state will have all the advantages and protection of citizens in the other states.

If somebody is charged with a crime in one state, then runs from the police to another state, the governor of the state in which the crime was committed can demand the return of that person, and the other state must obey.

A slave in one state, who escapes to a state where slavery is outlawed, will be returned to the slave owner upon their request.

Law or Regulation therein, be discharged from such Service or Labour but shall be delivered up on Claim of the Party to whom such Service or Labour may be due.

SECTION 3. New States may be admitted by the Congress into this Union; but no new State shall be formed or erected within the Jurisdiction of any other State; nor any State be formed by the Junction of two or more States; or Parts of States, without the Consent of the Legislatures of the States concerned as well as of the Congress.

The Congress shall have Power to dispose of and make all needful Rules and Regulations respecting the Territory or other Property belonging to the United States; and nothing in this Constitution shall be so construed as to Prejudice any claims of the United States, or of any particular State.

SECTION 4. The United States shall guarantee to every State in this Union a Republican Form of Government, and shall protect each of them against Invasion; and on Application of the Legislature, or of the Executive (when the Legislature cannot be convened) against domestic Violence.

ARTICLE V

The Congress, whenever two thirds of both Houses shall deem it necessary, shall propose AMENDMENTs to this Constitution, or, on the Application of the Legislatures of two thirds of the several States, shall call a Convention for proposing AMENDMENTs, which, in either Case, shall be valid to all Intents and Purposes, as Part

(The Thirteenth Amendment outlawed slavery, making this part of the Constitution outdated.)

SECTION 3. Congress can let new states into the Union, but no states can be formed inside another state. States cannot be made of two or more states, or parts of states, unless both the state legislatures of those states and Congress agree to it.

Congress has the power to make rules and laws for lands and other property of the United States. Nothing in the Constitution can be used to influence any claims of the United States or any state.

SECTION 4. The United States guarantees every state a government elected by the citizens of that state; and, it will protect the states from attack. The United States will also protect the states from local fighting, or riots, if the state legislatures ask for it. The governor can ask for this protection if the legislature of that state is not meeting at the time the help is needed.

ARTICLE V

The Constitution can be amended in two ways. First, a two-thirds vote of Congress is needed, approving the wording of the proposed amendment, followed by three-fourths of the state legislatures approving the amendment. Or, legislatures of two-thirds of the states can call a big meeting called a Constitutional Convention.

of this Constitution, when ratified by the Legislatures of three fourths of the several States, or by Conventions in three fourths thereof, as the one or the other Mode of Ratification may be proposed by the Congress; Provided that no AMENDMENT which may be made prior to the Year One thousand eight hundred and eight shall in any Manner affect the first and fourth Clauses in the Ninth Section of the first Article; and that no State, without its Consent, shall be deprived of it's equal Suffrage in the Senate.

At this meeting, the states can propose amendments to the Constitution. Either way, the amendments will become officially part of the Constitution when three-fourths of the state legislatures approve them. Congress may suggest another way to approve them. No amendment made before the year 1808 can affect the slave trade or how taxes are figured.

ARTICLE VI

All Debts contracted and Engagements entered into, before the Adoption of this Constitution, shall be as valid against the United States under this Constitution, as under the Confederation.

This Constitution, and the Laws of the United States which shall be made in Pursuance thereof; and all Treaties made, or which shall be made, under the Authority of the United States, shall be the supreme Law of the Land; and the Judges in every State shall be bound thereby, any Thing in the Constitution or Laws of any State to the Contrary notwithstanding.

The Senators and Representatives before mentioned, and the Members of the several State Legislatures, and all executive and judicial Officers, both of the United

ARTICLE VI

All debts and promises made by the United States before the approval of this Constitution will still be enforced under this Constitution.

This Constitution, the laws of the United States, and the treaties of the United States are the absolute law of the land— and all judges must honor them, despite anything different in state constitutions or state laws.

All senators, representatives, members of state legislatures, executive and judicial officers, both of the United States and in the states themselves, are bound by their

States and of the several States, shall be bound by Oath or Affirmation, to support this Constitution; but no religious Test shall ever be required as a Qualification to any Office or public Trust under the United States.

word to support this Constitution. No religious test can ever be used in order to serve in public office.

ARTICLE VII

The Ratification of the Conventions of nine States, shall be sufficient for the Establishment of this Constitution between the States so ratifying the Same.
[sic] done in Convention by the Unanimous Consent of the States present the Seventeenth Day of September in the Year of our Lord one thousand seven hundred and Eighty seven and of the Independence of the United States of America the Twelfth. IN WITNESS whereof We have hereunto subscribed our names,

ARTICLE VII

The approval of the constitutional meetings in nine states will be enough to approve the creation of this Constitution between the states.

This agreement is made unanimously by the states present on September 17, 1787; twelve years after becoming independent.

To witness this document, we now sign our names,

Fast Fact

The U.S. Constitution is the shortest, and the oldest, Constitution of any government in the world.

Go. Washington, President and deputy from Virginia

[Signed also by the deputies of twelve States.]

New Hampshire: John Langdon, Nicholas Gilman

Massachusetts: Nathaniel Gorham, Rufus King

Connecticut: Wm. Saml. Johnson, Roger Sherman

New York: Alexander Hamilton

New Jersey: Wil: Livingston, David Brearley,
Wm. Paterson, Jona: Dayton

Pennsylvania: B Franklin, Thomas Mifflin, Robt. Morris, Geo. Clymer, Thos. FitzSimons,, Jared
Ingersol, James Wilson, Gouv Morris

Delaware: Geo: Read, Gunning Bedford jun, John Dickinson,
Richard Bassett, Jaco: Broom

Maryland: James McHenry, Dan of St Thos. Jenifer, Danl Carroll

Virginia: John Blair, James Madison Jr.,

North Carolina: Wm. Blount, Richd. Dobbs Spaight, Hu Williamson

South Carolina: J. Rutledge

Georgia: William Few, Abraham Baldwin

Fast Fact

The Constitutional Convention of 1787 was held to fix the Articles of Confederation, an organization of states that was not working. Instead, the Founders wrote a new Constitution with a much stronger national government.

AMENDMENTS TO THE UNITED STATES CONSTITUTION, PROPOSED BY CONGRESS, AND RATIFIED BY THE LEGISLATURES OF THE SEVERAL STATES, PURSUANT TO THE FIFTH ARTICLE OF THE ORIGINAL CONSTITUTION

AMENDMENTS TO THE UNITED STATES CONSTITUTION, SUGGESTED BY CONGRESS, AND APPROVED BY THE STATES, LIKE THE FIFTH ARTICLE OF THE ORIGINAL CONSTITUTION SAYS . . .

The first ten Amendments are also known as

"The Bill of Rights"

Amendment I
(December 15, 1791)

Congress shall make no law respecting an establishment of religion, or prohibiting the free exercise thereof; or abridging the freedom of speech, or of the press; or the right of the people peaceably to assemble, and to petition the Government for a redress of grievances.

Amendment 1
Individual freedoms

Congress cannot make any law to: create a government church, keep people from practicing any religion they please (or not), keep people from writing or saying what is on their minds, keep people from getting together peacefully, or keep people from asking the government to hear their complaints.

Amendment II
(December 15, 1791)

A well regulated Militia, being necessary to the security of a free State, the right of the people to keep and bear Arms, shall not be infringed.

Amendment 2
Gun ownership as foundation
for militias

Since we need a militia (National Guard) to protect the country, citizens can own firearms (guns).

Amendment III
(December 15, 1791)

No Soldier shall, in time of peace be quartered in any house, without the consent of the Owner, nor in time of war, but in a manner to be prescribed by law.

Amendment 3
Housing of soldiers

In peacetime, citizens do not have to let soldiers stay in their homes. If there is a war, citizens do not have to let soldiers stay in their homes, unless there is a law to describe how it should happen.

Amendment IV
(December 15, 1791)

The right of the people to be secure in their persons, houses, papers, and effects, against unreasonable searches and seizures, shall not be violated, and no Warrants shall issue, but upon probable cause, supported by Oath or affirmation, and particularly describing the place to be searched, and the persons or things to be seized.

Amendment 4
Right of privacy for people and property

People, and their houses, papers and other things they own, are protected from the police taking their property or looking at their property without a warrant (permission given by a judge). If there is a need to search or take property, a judge must issue a warrant for a very good reason, supported by an oath, and the warrant must describe what is being looked at and what is being taken.

Amendment V
(December 15, 1791)

No person shall be held to answer for a capital, or otherwise infamous crime, unless on a presentment or indictment of a Grand Jury, except in cases arising in the land or naval forces, or in the Militia, when in actual service in time of War or public danger; nor shall any person be subject for the same offence to be twice put in jeopardy of life or limb, nor shall be compelled in any criminal case to be a witness against himself, nor be deprived of life, liberty, or property, without due

Amendment 5
Rights of individuals in criminal cases

Civilians cannot be made to defend themselves against a crime the government says he or she committed under federal law, unless a group of people (called a grand jury) agree that the charge is real. Then, that citizen can be officially accused (charged with a crime). Cases involving the armed forces or the National Guard are exceptions during wartime. No citizen can be held responsible for the same crime more than once. No citizen can be made to testify against himself or herself, and the

process of law; nor shall private property be taken for public use without just compensation.

government cannot take away a citizen's life, freedom, or property without applying the law. Private property cannot be taken for public use without a fair payment being made to its owner.

Amendment VI
(December 15, 1791)

In all criminal prosecutions, the accused shall enjoy the right to a speedy and public trial, by an impartial jury of the State and district wherein the crime shall have been committed; which district shall have been previously ascertained by law, and to be informed of the nature and cause of the accusation; to be confronted with the witnesses against him; to have compulsory process for obtaining witnesses in his favor, and to have the assistance of counsel for his defence.

Amendment 6
Rights for a fair trial

In criminal trials, a citizen blamed for a crime has the right to a quick, public trial; decided by an open-minded jury; in the general place (district) where the crime was committed—these places are determined by law. A citizen blamed for a crime must be told what the crime is that he or she is being blamed for, and why he or she is being blamed. The citizen blamed for a crime has the right to face the witnesses against him or her (the person or people who said this person did something wrong), and to be allowed to bring witnesses on his or her side (people who say the person didn't do anything wrong) into court, and to have a lawyer for his or her defense.

Amendment VII
(December 15, 1791)

In Suits at common law, where the value in controversy shall exceed twenty dollars, the right of trial by jury shall be preserved, and no fact tried by a jury shall be otherwise re-examined in any Court of the United States, than according to the rules of the common law.

Amendment 7
Rights in civil cases

In common law cases where somebody sues someone else for more than twenty dollars, that person has a right to a trial by jury. No fact examined by a jury can be re-examined in any court, except according to the current rules.

Fast Fact

The entire Constitution is only 4,440 words.

Amendment VIII
(December 15, 1791)

Excessive bail shall not be required, nor excessive fines imposed, nor cruel and unusual punishments inflicted.

Amendment 8
Bails, fines punishments

Citizens accused of a crime will not be required to pay bail that is out of proportion to the crime. Fines (money) charged to punish criminals must be reasonable, and any other punishment must not be cruel or unusual.

Amendment IX
(December 15, 1791)

The enumeration in the Constitution of certain rights shall not be construed to deny or disparage others retained by the people.

Amendment 9
Rights retained by the people

Just because some rights are listed in the Constitution does not mean that United States citizens do not have other rights.

Amendment X
(December 15, 1791)

The powers not delegated to the United States by the Constitution, nor prohibited by it to the States, are reserved to the States respectively, or to the people.

Amendment 10
Powers retained by the states
and the people

Powers not given to the United States by the Constitution, or powers denied to the federal government by the states, are given to the states and/or to the people themselves.

Amendment XI
(February 7, 1795)

The Judicial power of the United States shall not be construed to extend to any suit in law or equity, commenced or prosecuted against one of the United States by Citizens of another State, or by Citizens or Subjects of any Foreign State.

Amendment XII
(June 15, 1804)

The Electors shall meet in their respective states, and vote by ballot for President and Vice-President, one of whom, at least, shall not be an inhabitant of the same state with themselves; they shall name in their ballots the person voted for as President, and in distinct ballots the person voted for as Vice-President, and they shall make distinct lists of all persons voted for as President, and of all persons voted for as Vice-President, and of the number of votes for each, which lists they shall sign and certify, and transmit sealed to the seat of the government of the United States, directed to the President of the Senate;—The President of the Senate shall, in the presence of the Senate and House of Representatives, open all the certificates and the votes shall then be counted;—The person having the greatest number of votes for President, shall be the President, if such number be a

Amendment 11
Lawsuits against states

No one can use the power of the Courts against a state unless that person lives in that state. Citizens of another country cannot use the courts to sue any of the states.

Amendment 12
Election of the President and Vice President

The electors meet in their home states and vote for the President and the Vice President using a ballot. An elector cannot vote for a President and a Vice President if both are from the same state as the elector. On the ballots, the electors must clearly mark their choice for President and Vice President. Then, the electors make a list of all the candidates who were voted for as President and Vice President, including how many votes each candidate got.

The electors then sign and approve each list, seal it and send it to the United States Congress in Washington, D.C., to the attention of the President of the Senate. The President of the Senate opens it in front of the House of Representatives and the Senate, and counts all the votes. The person who has a majority of electoral votes will be the President of the United States.

majority of the whole number of Electors appointed; and if no person have such majority, then from the persons having the highest numbers not exceeding three on the list of those voted for as President, the House of Representatives shall choose immediately, by ballot, the President. But in choosing the President, the votes shall be taken by states, the representation from each state having one vote; a quorum for this purpose shall consist of a member or members from two-thirds of the states, and a majority of all the states shall be necessary to a choice. And if the House of Representatives shall not choose a President whenever the right of choice shall devolve upon them, before the fourth day of March next following, then the Vice-President shall act as President, as in the case of the death or other constitutional disability of the President. The person having the greatest number of votes as Vice-President, shall be the Vice-President, if such number be a majority of the whole number of Electors appointed, and if no person have a majority, then from the two highest numbers on the list, the Senate shall choose the Vice-President; a quorum for the purpose shall consist of two-thirds of the whole number of Senators, and a majority of the whole number shall be necessary to a choice. But no person constitutionally ineligible to the office of President shall be eligible to that of Vice-President of the United States.

If no candidate gets a majority of electoral votes, then the House of Representatives picks the President by casting their vote for one of the top three presidential candidates who got the most electoral votes. The delegation (all the representatives from a state) of each state will have only one vote. A quorum (the least amount of people needed to make a decision) will be at least one member from two-thirds of the states voting. A majority (fifty percent plus one) of all the states will be required to make this decision. If the representatives fool around and do not make a decision before March 4 of the next year, then the Vice President becomes the President, just like if the President was to die, or be unable to serve. (The Twentieth Amendment added a little more about this.)

The person with the majority of electoral votes for Vice President will be the Vice President. If no candidate gets a majority of electoral votes, then the Senate picks the Vice President by ballot from the two Vice Presidential candidates who have the most electoral votes. At least two-thirds of the senators are needed to make this decision; and a majority (fifty percent plus one) of the Senate will be required to make the final choice. The constitutional guidelines for the President are the same for the Vice President.

Amendment XIII
(December 6, 1865)

SECTION 1. Neither slavery nor involuntary servitude, except as a punishment for crime whereof the party shall have been duly convicted, shall exist within the United States, or any place subject to their jurisdiction.

SECTION 2. Congress shall have power to enforce this article by appropriate legislation.

Amendment 13
Abolishment of Slavery

SECTION 1. Slavery no longer exists in the United States, or in any of the places the United States controls. No one is forced to work for anyone else for no pay, except as punishment for a crime that the criminal has been convicted of by a court of law.

SECTION 2. Congress has the power to enforce this Amendment with laws.

Amendment XIV
(July 9, 1868)

SECTION 1. All persons born or naturalized in the United States and subject to the jurisdiction thereof, are citizens of the United States and of the State wherein they reside. No State shall make or enforce any law which shall abridge the privileges or immunities of citizens of the United States; nor shall any State deprive any person of life, liberty, or property, without due process of law; nor deny to any person within its jurisdiction the equal protection of the laws.

Amendment 14
Equal protection under the law for everyone

SECTION 1. Anyone born in the United States, or given citizenship by the United States, is a citizen of the United States and citizens of the state where they live. States cannot make or enforce any laws that limit the rewards or protections of any citizen of the United States. No state can take away any citizen's life, freedom, or belongings without proper use of the law. Every person is given the same protection under the law.

SECTION 2. Representatives shall be apportioned among the several States according to their respective numbers, counting the whole number of persons in each State, excluding Indians not taxed. But when the right to vote at any election for the choice of electors for President and Vice President of the United States, Representatives in Congress, the Executive and Judicial officers of a State, or the members of the Legislature thereof, is denied to any of the male inhabitants of such State, being twenty-one years of age, and citizens of the United States, or in any way abridged, except for participation in rebellion, or other crime, the basis of representation therein shall be reduced in the proportion which the number of such male citizens shall bear to the whole number of male citizens twenty one years of age in such State.

SECTION 3. No person shall be a Senator or Representative in Congress, or elector of President and Vice President, or hold any office, civil or military, under the United States, or under any State, who, having previously taken an oath, as a member of Congress, or as an officer of the United States, or as a member of any State legislature, or as an executive or judicial officer of any State, to support the Constitution of the United States, shall have engaged in insurrection or rebellion against the same, or given aid or comfort to the enemies thereof. But Congress may by a vote of two-thirds of each House, remove such disability.

SECTION 4. The validity of the public debt of the United States, authorized by law, including debts incurred for payment of pensions and bounties for services in suppressing insurrection or rebellion, shall not be questioned. But neither the

SECTION 2. The number of representatives in the House of Representatives is determined by the number of people living in the states, except Native Americans who are not taxed. If a state does not let a male citizen over twenty-one years old vote freely (unless he commits a crime, or takes part in a rebellion), the number of representatives for that state will be reduced.

SECTION 3. No one can be a senator, representative, elector or officer of the United States—or United States military officer, or member of a state legislature, or a governor, or a judge of any state—if they took an oath to support the Constitution and then took part in a rebellion (a fight) against the United States, or gave aid and comfort to the enemies of the United States. But Congress can change this with a two-thirds vote.

SECTION 4. Any money the United States owes for paying pensions, or for paying for help to stop a revolt, can not be questioned. Neither the United States nor any state can pay any money to anyone for help in rebelling against the United States, and

United States nor any State shall assume or pay any debt or obligation incurred in aid of insurrection or rebellion against the United States, or any claim for the loss or emancipation of any slave; but all such debts, obligations and claims shall be held illegal and void.

no state or the United States can pay for a lost or freed slave—in fact all such bills, obligations and claims are not legal.

SECTION 5. The Congress shall have power to enforce, by appropriate legislation, the provisions of this article.

SECTION 5. Congress has the power to enforce this Amendment by law.

Amendment XV
(February 3, 1870)

Amendment 15
Voting rights

SECTION 1. The right of citizens of the United States to vote shall not be denied or abridged by the United States or by any State on account of race, color, or previous condition of servitude.

SECTION 1. The United States, or any state, cannot deny anyone the right to vote based on their race, the color of their skin, or the fact that they were once a slave.

SECTION 2. The Congress shall have power to enforce this article by appropriate legislation.

SECTION 2. Congress has the power to enforce this Amendment by law.

Fast Fact

On September 17, 1787, the Continental Congress approved the Constitution.

Amendment XVI
(February 3, 1913)

The Congress shall have power to lay and collect taxes on incomes, from whatever source derived, without apportionment among the several States, and without regard to any census or enumeration.

Amendment 16
Congress' power to tax

Congress has the power to place and collect taxes on citizens' incomes (income taxes) without regard to the states, or without counting people.

Amendment XVII
(April 8, 1913)

The Senate of the United States shall be composed of two Senators from each State, elected by the people thereof, for six years; and each Senator shall have one vote. The electors in each State shall have the qualifications requisite for electors of the most numerous branch of the State legislatures.

When vacancies happen in the representation of any State in the Senate, the executive authority of each State shall issue writs of election to fill such vacancies: Provided, That the legislature of any State may empower the executive thereof to make temporary appointments until the people fill the vacancies by election as the legislature may direct.

This AMENDMENT shall not be so construed as to affect the election or term of any Senator chosen before it becomes valid as part of the Constitution.

Amendment 17
Direct election of U.S. Senators

The Senate of the United States is made up of two senators from each state, elected by the people in that state every six years. Each senator has one vote. The electors in each state must have the same qualifications as electors of the biggest house of the state legislature.

If a senator dies or leaves office, the governor of that state calls for an election to elect a new senator. The state legislature can let the governor appoint somebody to be the "temporary" senator until that election is held.

This Amendment will not change the election or term of any senators until it becomes a valid part of the Constitution.

Amendment XVIII
(January 16, 1919)

SECTION 1. After one year from the ratification of this article the manufacture, sale, or transportation of intoxicating liquors within, the importation thereof into, or the exportation thereof from the United States and all territory subject to the jurisdiction thereof for beverage purposes is hereby prohibited.

SECTION 2. The Congress and the several States shall have concurrent power to enforce this article by appropriate legislation.

SECTION 3. This article shall be inoperative unless it shall have been ratified as an AMENDMENT to the Constitution by the legislatures of the several States, as provided in the Constitution, within seven years from the date of the submission hereof to the States by the Congress.

Amendment 18
Prohibition of alcohol

SECTION 1. One year after this Amendment is official, nobody can make, sell, or move beer, wine, or liquor anywhere in the United States—or anywhere under the control of the United States.

(This Amendment was later repealed.)

SECTION 2. Congress and the states have the power to enforce this Amendment by law.

SECTION 3. This Amendment will not work unless it is approved and added to the Constitution by the state legislatures, like the Constitution says, in seven years from the day it is given to the states by Congress.

Amendment XIX
(August 18, 1920)

The right of citizens of the United States to vote shall not be denied or abridged by the United States or by any State on account of sex.

Congress shall have power to enforce this article by appropriate legislation.

Amendment 19
Women get the right to vote

Women have the right to vote. The right to vote cannot be denied because of someone's sex.

Congress can enforce this Amendment by law.

Amendment XX
(January 23, 1933)

SECTION 1. The terms of the President and Vice President shall end at noon on the 20th day of January, and the terms of Senators and Representatives at noon on the 3rd day of January, of the years in which such terms would have ended if this article had not been ratified; and the terms of their successors shall then begin.

SECTION 2. The Congress shall assemble at least once in every year, and such meeting shall begin at noon on the 3rd day of January, unless they shall by law appoint a different day.

SECTION 3. If, at the time fixed for the beginning of the term of the President, the President elect shall have died, the Vice President elect shall become President. If a President shall not have been chosen before the time fixed for the beginning of his term, or if the President elect shall have failed to qualify, then the Vice President elect shall act as President until a President shall have qualified; and the Congress may by law provide for the case wherein neither a President elect nor a Vice President elect shall have qualified, declaring who shall then act as President, or the manner in which one who is to act shall be selected, and such person shall act accordingly until a President or Vice President shall have qualified.

SECTION 4. The Congress may by law provide for the case of the death of any of the persons from whom the House of Representatives may choose a President whenever the right of choice shall have

Amendment 20
Terms of the President, Vice President and Congress

SECTION 1. Terms of the President and the Vice President end at noon on January 20. Terms of senators and representatives will begin and end at noon on January 3.

SECTION 2. Congress must meet at least once every year, starting on January 3, unless they pass a law to pick another day.

SECTION 3. If the President-Elect dies after the election and before noon on January 20, the Vice President-Elect becomes President. If, for some reason, a President is not chosen before January 20, or if the President-Elect does not meet the rules laid out in the Constitution, then the Vice President-Elect will act as President until someone is chosen as President. If neither the President-Elect nor the Vice President-Elect meets the rules laid out in the Constitution, the Congress can decide, by law, who will act as President, and how a President should then be picked. That person will act as President until the constitutional rules can be followed.

SECTION 4. If the representatives ever have to choose a President, or the senators ever have to choose a Vice President, and that person dies before they take office, the Congress can make a law to deal with that.

devolved upon them, and for the case of the death of any of the persons from whom the Senate may choose a Vice President whenever the right of choice shall have devolved upon them.

SECTION 5. Sections 1 and 2 shall take effect on the 15th day of October following the ratification of this article.

SECTION 6. This article shall be inoperative unless it shall have been ratified as an AMENDMENT to the Constitution by the legislatures of three fourths of the several States within seven years from the date of its submission.

SECTION 5. Section 1 and 2 will take effect on October 15 after this Amendment becomes part of the Constitution.

SECTION 6. This Amendment will not work unless it is approved and added to the Constitution by the state legislatures, like the Constitution says, seven years from the day after it is given to the states by Congress.

Amendment XXI
(December 5, 1933)

Amendment 21
Repeal of the 18th Amendment

SECTION 1. The eighteenth article of AMENDMENT to the Constitution of the United States is hereby repealed.

SECTION 2. The transportation or importation into any State, Territory, or possession of the United States for delivery or use therein of intoxicating liquors, in violation of the laws thereof, is hereby prohibited.

SECTION 3. This article shall be inoperative unless it shall have been ratified as an AMENDMENT to the Constitution by conventions in the several States, as provided in the Constitution, within seven years from the date of the submission hereof to the States by the Congress.

SECTION 1. The eighteenth Amendment is repealed (thrown out).

SECTION 2. States, territories, or other areas under the control of the United States can still pass laws making it illegal to make, sell, move, or drink beer, wine, or liquor.

SECTION 3. This Amendment will not work unless it is approved and added to the Constitution by the state legislatures, like the Constitution says, seven years from the day after it is given to the states by Congress.

Amendment XXII
(February 27, 1951)

SECTION 1. No person shall be elected to the office of the President more than twice, and no person who has held the office of President, or acted as President, for more than two years of a term to which some other person was elected President shall be elected to the office of President more than once. But this Article shall not apply to any person holding the office of President when this Article was proposed by the Congress, and shall not prevent any person who may be holding the office of President, or acting as President, during the term within which this Article becomes operative from holding the office of President or acting as President during the remainder of such term.

SECTION 2. This article shall be inoperative unless it shall have been ratified as an AMENDMENT to the Constitution by the legislatures of three-fourths of the several States within seven years from the date of its submission to the States by the Congress.

Amendment XXIII
(March 29, 1961)

SECTION 1. The District constituting the seat of Government of the United States shall appoint in such manner as the Congress may direct:

A number of electors of President and Vice President equal to the whole number of Senators and Representatives in Congress to which the District would be entitled if

Amendment 22
Limit of Presidential terms

SECTION 1. Nobody can be elected President more than twice. Nobody who has held the office of President, or acted as President, for more than two years of someone else's term, can be elected more than once. This Amendment does not affect the President now, and it does not affect anyone who may act as President until this Amendment is officially approved and added to the Constitution.

SECTION 2. This Amendment will not work unless it is approved and added to the Constitution by the state legislatures, like the Constitution says, seven years from the day after it is given to the states by Congress.

Amendment 23
Washington, D.C. electors
for President

SECTION 1. The place where the seat of government is located (now it is Washington, the District of Columbia) can pick electors like this:

The number of electors is figured as if the District of Columbia was a state, and the number would equal the number of senators and representatives of the smallest

it were a State, but in no event more than the least populous State; they shall be in addition to those appointed by the States, but they shall be considered, for the purposes of the election of President and Vice President, to be electors appointed by a State; and they shall meet in the District and perform such duties as provided by the twelfth article of AMENDMENT.

SECTION 2. The Congress shall have the power to enforce this article by appropriate legislation.

state. These electors would be in addition to the electors chosen by the states. For the election of the President and Vice President, electors act like they are from a state. They meet in the District of Columbia and follow the rules of the Twelfth Amendment.

SECTION 2. Congress has the power to enforce this Amendment by law.

Amendment XXIV
(January 23, 1964)

SECTION 1. The right of citizens of the United States to vote in any primary or other election for President or Vice President, for electors for President or Vice President, or for Senator or Representative in Congress, shall not be denied or abridged by the United States or any State by reason of failure to pay any poll tax or other tax.

SECTION 2. The Congress shall have the power to enforce this article by appropriate legislation.

Amendment 24
Elimination of the poll tax

SECTION 1. No state can make people pay a tax in order to vote in any election for President, Vice President, senator or representative.

SECTION 2. Congress has the power to enforce this Amendment by law.

Amendment XXV
(February 10, 1967)

SECTION 1. In case of the removal of the President from office or of his death or resignation, the Vice President shall become President.

SECTION 2. Whenever there is a vacancy in the office of the Vice President, the President shall nominate a Vice President who shall take office upon confirmation by a majority vote of both Houses of Congress.

SECTION 3. Whenever the President transmits to the President pro tempore of the Senate and the Speaker of the House of Representatives his written declaration that he is unable to discharge the powers and duties of his office, and until he transmits to them a written declaration to the contrary, such powers and duties shall be discharged by the Vice President as Acting President.

SECTION 4. Whenever the Vice President and a majority of either the principal officers of the executive departments or of such other body as Congress may by law provide, transmit to the President pro tempore of the Senate and the Speaker of the House of Representatives their written declaration that the President is unable to discharge the power and duties of his office, the Vice President shall immediately assume the powers and duties of the office as Acting President.

Amendment 25
Succession of office

SECTION 1. If the President dies, leaves office, or gets kicked out (impeached), the Vice President becomes the President.

SECTION 2. If for some reason there is not a Vice President, the President picks one, and that person becomes the Vice President after a majority of senators and representatives approve that person.

SECTION 3. If the President writes to the President of the Senate and the Speaker of the House of Representatives and tells him or her they believe the President can no longer do the job—the Vice President becomes the Acting President. The President who gave up the office has to write to the President of the Senate and the Speaker of the House again to let them know when he or she thinks they can do the job again.

SECTION 4. If the Vice President and a majority of the Cabinet officers write to the President of the Senate and the Speaker of the House to tell them the President cannot do the job, the Vice President immediately begins acting as President.

Thereafter, when the President transmits to the President pro tempore of the Senate and the Speaker of the House of Representatives his written declaration that no inability exists, he shall resume the powers and duties of his office unless the Vice President and a majority of either the principal officers of the executive department or of such other body as Congress may by law provide, transmit within four days to the President pro tempore of the Senate and the Speaker of the House of Representatives their written declaration that the President is unable to discharge the powers and duties of his office. Thereupon Congress shall decide the issue, assembling within forty-eight hours for that purpose if not in session. If the Congress, within twenty-one days after receipt of the latter written declaration, or, if Congress is not in session, within twenty-one days after Congress is required to assemble, determines by two-thirds vote of both Houses that the President is unable to discharge the powers and duties of his office, the Vice President shall continue to discharge the same as Acting President; otherwise, the President shall resume the powers and duties of his office.

When the original President writes to the President of the Senate and the Speaker of the House to tell them he or she can now do the job again, the President immediately gets back the powers as President—unless within four days, the Vice President and a majority of the Cabinet officers write the President of the Senate and the Speaker of the House and tells them they don't think the President is ready to resume his or her duties. If all that happens, Congress will meet within forty-eight hours to decide the issue. Congress must act within twenty-one days of receiving the letter. If senators and representatives decide by a two-thirds vote that the original President cannot do the job, the Vice President will continue to act as President. Otherwise, the President gets the job back.

Amendment XXVI
(July 1, 1971)

SECTION 1. The right of citizens of the United States, who are eighteen years of age or older, to vote shall not be denied or abridged by the United States or by any State on account of age.

SECTION 2. The Congress shall have the power to enforce this article by appropriate legislation.

Amendment 26
Right of 18-year-old citizens to vote

SECTION 1. Citizens who are eighteen years old can now vote. The United States, or any state, cannot take away anyone's right to vote based on age.

SECTION 2. Congress has the power to enforce this Amendment by law.

Amendment XXVII
(May 7, 1992)

(Article the Second . . .) No law, varying the compensation for the services of the Senators and Representatives, shall take effect, until an election of Representatives shall have intervened.

Amendment 27
Determination of Congressional pay raises

Congress cannot get a raise until an election is held after they passed the law giving themselves a raise.

Fast Fact

James Madison was known as the "Father of our Constitution." He had more to do with creating it than anybody else. He was later elected and served as the fourth President of the United States from 1809-1817.

Dividing It Up

The Founders didn't really trust any government, not the one they had just defeated (British) or the one they were creating. They were smart about people and wanted to factor in the human failings of those who would be in the government.

Probably the smartest thing these men did when writing the Constitution was to divide up the power of the federal government three ways, plus give the states a great deal of power.

The first three Articles of the Constitution set up this unique power-sharing idea. The Founders divided the government into a Congress (legislative), a President (executive) and a judiciary (judges) branch. They had to make all three of them equal, or it wouldn't work. By dividing the government into three separate parts (branches), they made sure that the power of the United States government was never in the hands of just one person, or one group of people. This is called "separation of powers."

This separation of powers is one of the foundations of the U.S. Constitution. Congress makes laws with the President and an independent group of judges (the Supreme Court) keeps an eye on everybody. The Supreme Court is the final word on how the Constitution applies to questions of law.

Here's how the three branches of government act together:

- Congress passes laws, but the President can veto those laws.

- Congress can get by (overrule) a presidential veto if two-thirds of both the House of Representatives and the Senate agree.

- Only Congress can make an army or declare war, but the President is the Commander-in-Chief of the armed forces.

- The President appoints all federal judges, ambassadors and some other important officials, but the Senate must approve of all of his or her appointments.

- The Supreme Court has the final power to strike down both congressional and presidential acts as unconstitutional.

- To impeach a President, the accusation must pass the full House of Representatives; the Senate decides the guilt or innocence of the President at a trial with the Chief Justice of the Supreme Court presiding.

This balancing of power makes sure no one branch controls the federal government.

Fast Fact

When the Continental Congress first printed copies of the Constitution, they told the printer to print just a few copies. The draft was kept secret to avoid controversy.

Constitutional Compromises

---

com·pro·mise n. — 1. A settlement of differences in which each side makes concessions. 2. The result of such a settlement. 3. A middle way between two extremes. 4. Something that combines qualities or elements of different things. Origins: Latin, compr-missum, or mutual promise.

When deciding how many people would represent each state in Congress, the Founders argued that large states (states with more people) would run right over small states (states with fewer people). So they compromised, basing membership in the House of Representatives on population alone (determined by the census) and sending two senators per state to the Senate, so all states have an equal say in the Senate.

Southern states with many slaveholders (slaves were considered property when the Constitution was written) worried that their small population would earn them very small groups to go to the House of Representatives. They compromised on how to count slaves as part of their state's population (take the overall population of slaves in a state and count three-fifths of that group to figure out the state's representation in Congress).

To make sure states had a voice in electing the President (and because they never really thought the general population could make a good choice), the Founders created the Electoral College, a group of people from each state that would cast the final votes for President and Vice President of the United States.

Since the Constitution Was Written . . .

Since the Founders wrote the Constitution so long ago, Congress has passed a lot of new laws about nearly everything.

We selected our forty-third President at the dawn of the twenty-first century. Some Presidents have been pretty good; others have been average. President Abraham Lincoln kept the states together as a country during and after the Civil War. President John F. Kennedy kept the nation out of a nuclear war in 1962. But the enduring magic of our system of government is that power is surrendered peacefully after each of our elections.

This century has already seen several different Congresses; and Congress is always in an argument with the President to see who has the most power.

It is the job of Congress to spend the money that people pay to support the government (taxes). The President can tell Congress how he or she wants to spend the money, but Congress has the final say.

Our most basic political struggle continues to be about the power of the federal government and the power of the states . . . that was true when the country was born, it was true at our worst moment (the Civil War), and it is true today. The Civil War tragically divided us on the question of power, and the federal government won. But the power of the states was apparent in the success Southern states had keeping African Americans from voting from 1865 until 1965, exactly one hundred years after the Civil War was over.

The Supreme Court has made a bunch of decisions in arguments between citizens, states and the government of the United States. Some of today's laws come from decisions that the Supreme Court has made over the last two hundred years. Although the Constitution always said that all citizens were equal, it was only about fifty years ago that the Supreme Court finally started deciding cases that really began to treat all people equally.

People are always going to disagree with the government, just because they have a right to do that. That is a very precious right, and we must always protect it and exercise it. People in this country can say just about anything they want, about anything or anybody they want, and the First Amendment will protect them. They may not be right, they may not be nice, they may not even make any sense, but they can always say what they wish.

To be part of our history, remember what is in the Constitution and make sure that your rights and liberties are exercised and protected, as well as those of your family and friends. The Constitution governs everyone who lives in the United States, not just the adults. It only works when people know what it means.

Use the information in *Constitution Translated for Kids* to know what to expect from your government right now, and to understand the liberties and responsibilities of living in the United States of America.

Fast Fact

The Federal Convention convened in the State House (Independence Hall) in Philadelphia on May 14, 1787.

Words to Look at While You Are Reading

This list does not include all the hard words in the original text of the Constitution, only the ones in this translation.

Amended — If a law is amended, that means we just added more to it, or made it different in some way.

Appointed — In the United States, people who are picked by the President to serve in the government or on the courts, are "appointed" to those positions.

Bail — This is the money people pay to get out of jail while they wait for their trial to begin.

Ballot — A ballot is a little piece of paper on which people write down their votes (most people cast electronic ballots now). Presidential electors still use paper ballots (which are constitutionally mandated).

Bill, Act, Law — If someone in Congress has an idea for a law, they write it down for everybody to read. It is called a "bill," or an "act." After a bill has been passed by Congress and signed by the President, it is the law.

Cabinet — The Cabinet is made up of people the President picks to be in charge of the different departments in the government. In the United States, the people in the President's Cabinet are his or her official advisors.

Candidate — A candidate is someone who runs for any kind of office.

Case — A case is a set of circumstances that need to be investigated. When people are accused of a crime and they have to go to court, they are part of a case. The case (or circumstance) is what the people, and the person blamed for the crime, tell the judge and the jury.

Census — The census is the official count of people in this country; we take it every ten years.

Citizen, Citizenship — When you are born in a country, you are a citizen of that country. Citizenship is what you have if you are a citizen. If you weren't born in the United States, you have to live in the U.S. for a while and take a test before you can become a citizen. If your parents are both United States citizens, and you are born in another country, you are automatically a United States citizen.

Constitution — The word itself actually means to set things up and get things started. In the United States, the Constitution got the United States government all set up.

Delegation — A delegation is a group of people that officially represents other people.

Democracy — Democracy is a form of government where all the people in the country have the power to vote for the people who make the laws. It is a government by the people.

Elections, Elected — Elections are when people vote for their leaders. The candidates with the most votes are elected. In presidential races, the person with the most electoral votes wins the office.

Elector, Electoral College — An elector is one of a small group of people in a state who vote for the President and Vice President. When citizens vote for President and Vice President, they are actually voting for electors. The Electoral College is made up of all the electors from the fifty states and the District of Columbia (Washington, D.C.). The Electoral College exists only once every four years for the sole purpose of electing a President and Vice President.

Empower — Empower means to give someone the power to do something.

Enforce — Enforce means to make someone mind and follow the rules.

Federal — The United States has several levels of government. There are local governments (cities and towns); there are state governments; and, there is the federal government. The federal government, located in Washington, D.C., is the government the Constitution set up.

Founders — Founders are the people who get a country or a movement started. In the United States, the Founders were a group of men whose families came from Europe, and who wanted to start a new country

Governor — In the United States, a governor is the top person in charge of a state.

Grand Jury — This is a small group of people gathered together by the local authorities to decide if there is enough evidence to try someone for a crime.

Impeach, Impeachment — The word "impeach" actually means to discredit. In the United States government, impeaching someone begins the process of kicking them out of office. "Impeachment" is the process that leads to kicking someone out of office. If someone is "impeached," they are accused of doing something wrong by the House of Representatives. The Senate can then hold the "impeachment trial" to either kick that person out of office, or decide that that person does not deserve to get kicked out. The House acts as a grand jury; and, the Senate acts as a jury for impeachment cases.

Income — Income is the money people make from working.

Journal — A journal is sort of like a diary. It is the official record of daily meetings in Congress.

Judge(s) — A judge is a person who hears cases in court. Judges are always in charge in a courtroom. They give directions to the people talking (lawyers and witnesses) and to the jury that decides the case.

Jury — A jury is a group of people who don't know the person on trial, and who settle arguments between people in a case in court.

Legislature — The legislature is an elected group of people who makes laws. In the United States, each state has a legislature. The country's legislature is the Congress.

Officers — An officer is someone who holds an office of trust in the civilian government. Officers are also people in the military who are in charge of other military people.

Override — When Congress votes with two-thirds of its members present, it can override a President's veto of a law Congress has passed. If Congress is successful in their "veto override," the bill in question becomes law anyway.

Quorum — A quorum is the least amount of people needed in order to do business in Congress.

Ratify, Ratified — To formally approve something, or give legal power to something, is to ratify it.

Repealed — If a law is repealed, it is completely erased. It is no longer a law.

Supreme — "Supreme" means highest. The Supreme Court is the highest court in the land. The supreme law of the United States is the Constitution. No law is more powerful; it is the highest law in the nation.

Tax, Taxed — A tax is money that people pay to support the government. People who make money legally are "taxed."

Treason, Crimes — Crimes are actions that break the law. Treason is a really bad crime because it is a crime against everybody in the country. The Constitution lays out a very clear explanation of treason (Article III, Section 3).

Trial, Try — A trial is the courtroom contest between the person blamed for the crime and the accusers. It is held in front of a judge and jury. To "try" somebody means to have a trial.

Veto — The word itself means to forbid; a veto is an official act that forbids something. In the Constitution, if the President opposes a law passed by Congress, it is vetoed.

Warrant — Warrants are orders judges give police if they think someone is breaking the law—the warrant allows police to search private homes, or arrest somebody.

Fast Fact

On July 2, 1788, the Continental Congress heard that New Hampshire had just become the ninth state to ratify the new Constitution, making it the law of the land.

Overview of the Constitution

The Constitution belongs to: "We the people"—that means everyone in the country.

The Constitution set up three branches of government:

- Legislative (Congress),

- Executive (President),

- and, Judiciary (Supreme Court and other federal courts).

There are seven Articles in the Constitution and twenty-seven Amendments.

Fast Fact

The Constitution was created by many people, and is a model for the "art of compromise" among many different people with many different opinions and ideas.

Congress

Congress consists of two parts: the House of Representatives and the Senate. The number of members in the House of Representatives (four hundred thirty-five) is based on the nation's population. There are one hundred senators, two per state.

The Vice President of the United States is the President of the Senate; the top officer for the House of Representatives is the Speaker of the House. Neither the House of Representatives nor the Senate can adjourn (leave) unless they both agree to do so.

Bills that raise taxes ALWAYS begin in the House of Representatives.

There are two ways for a bill to become a law:

1. Congress must pass it, and the President must sign it; or,

2. Congress must pass it, and if the President vetoes it (basically says "no"), Congress can override the veto with two-thirds of the members voting to override.

Congress generally makes laws (in consultation with the President who must sign them). Here are some of the specific powers the Constitution gives to Congress (a complete listing is in Article I, Section 8):

- Raise/spend money;

- Print/establish worth of money;

- Fix a system of weights, measurements;

- Promote science, unique works by issuing copyrights;

- Make war;

- Make all the rules for the army and navy (but the President is the Commander-in-Chief); and,

- Make laws for the entire country.

Members of the House of Representatives must be at least twenty-five years old; senators must be at least thirty years old.

Executive Branch (Presidency)

The President (Chief Executive) is the one person who is ultimately in charge of the country.

When people vote for president, they aren't really voting for a person running for president; they vote for Electors, the people who make up the Electoral College. The Electoral College is a small group of people from all the states that cast the official votes for the President and Vice-President in an election. (Further discussion of the modern Electoral College, or "electors," is in the 12th Amendment.)

If something happens to the President, the Vice-President becomes the President.

Presidents must be born to citizens of the United States, so if U.S. citizens were in another country, and had their baby there, the child could grow up to be President of the United States. But if two people from another country moved here with their baby after the baby was born in that country, that child could not serve as President.

Other responsibilities the Constitution gives the President include (a full listing is in Article II, Section 2):

- Work with Congress to make laws;

- Act as Commander-in-Chief of the armed forces;

- Makes treaties (but needs advice and permission from the Senate); and,

- Appoint Supreme Court Justices, U.S. Ambassadors (but needs advice and permission from the Senate);

- Make a State of the Union speech (an update on where the country is and ideas for making it better); and,

- Ensure the laws are carried out equally for everyone.

When a President gets impeached by the House of Representatives, the President does not leave office because the impeachment hearings are only the beginning of the process. Two-thirds of the Senate must vote to remove a President from office after the House impeaches him or her.

The Constitution give some pretty important responsibilities to the President, but also makes some of them subject to the "advice and consent (permission)" of the Senate. The Founders, who fought a war for independence, and who lived under the control of one man, knew that all that power should never be in the hands of one person. Requiring the President to talk to Congress before he or she makes a decision creates a "check" on the person who serves as President—it "balances" out the power.

Examples of our system of "checks and balances" include:

- Three different branches of government (Legislative, Judicial and Executive);

- Requiring the "advice and consent" of the Senate when appointing Supreme Court Justices and other important officers; and,

- Giving Congress the power to override a veto with two-thirds of its members.

The Constitution insists that if Congress overrides a veto, they must do so with two-thirds of their members because they wanted the laws to withstand the hardest tests. So, if a bill that passes with a majority in Congress (over fifty percent of the members) gets vetoed, then the Constitution says Congress has to re-examine it, consider the President's objections, then vote on it again. But they need two-thirds of their members (in both the House of Representatives and the Senate) to approve the bill in order to overrule the President's objections and make it a law.

The Founders also knew that little groups of people could do as much damage as a single powerful person, so they worried a little bit about what majorities in Congress could do. Requiring Congress to override a veto with two-thirds of the membership took care of their concerns.

Fast Fact

The night the Continental Congress passed the Constitution, printers worked late into the night on the final imprint of the six-page Constitution, copies of which would leave Philadelphia early on the morning stagecoach to tell the world about the new government.

Judiciary

A Justice (Supreme or Federal Court judge) serves for his or her lifetime (barring impeachment). They settle arguments that cannot be solved in lower courts across the nation, or arguments directly involving the Constitution.

The Constitution defines treason (the act of a traitor) as making war against the United States, working with our enemies, or giving our enemies "aid and comfort." This is a very high standard. it is not something to say casually about somebody.

Fast Fact

The hot, muggy Philadelphia summer made the delegates irritable with each other. James Madison said the heat nearly killed him.

States

The Founders wanted the states to have a good deal of power. Each state has to honor the other states' acts, records and legal reports. Congress judges these records and laws in case they conflict with other records and laws.

If somebody commits a crime in one state, they cannot escape justice by going to another state because each state's justice reaches into all the other states.

Only Congress can decide how new states join the United States; and, no state can leave the United States after they join. We fought a Civil War over just that constitutional question.

Housekeeping

The Constitution is never finished . . . it is called a "living document." It can be changed, or perfected, by amendment; and has already been amended twenty-seven times.

To amend the Constitution, an amendment must be passed by two-thirds of the House of Representatives, two-thirds of the Senate and must be ratified (accepted) by three-fourths the states.

The Constitution is considered the "supreme law of the land." We require the elected or appointed officers of our government to support the Constitution with their word or oath. It is the only oath allowed under the Constitution. No religious test must ever be a qualifier for service in any government office.

Fast Fact

After they informally accepted the Constitution, and while it was being printed, New York's Governor Morris and George Washington rode along a creek by Valley Forge where ten years before the soldiers of the Continental Army suffered great hardships in the War of Independence. While Morris cast for trout, Washington remembered how far the country had travelled.

Amendments

The first ten Amendments to the Constitution talk about individual liberties for each person who lives in the country. They are known collectively as the Bill of Rights—they protect the most personal, individual rights of citizens. These individual rights were so important to our Founders that they put them in writing in order to guarantee people would forever understand their importance. In fact, some states didn't want to sign the Constitution until the Bill of Rights was added.

Interestingly, the Bill of Rights was originally meant to apply only to federal laws, but most of the Bill of Rights has been adopted by all the states.

First (I) Amendment
Individual Freedoms

Individual freedoms listed in the First Amendment include freedom of religion, speech, press, assembly (gathering together), and the right to take protests to Congress. People can say or write practically anything. If a TV reporter, or a newspaper, magazine or website says something untrue about someone or something very important and scares everybody, they are free to do that, and they sometimes do. Democracy demands that people use good sense to tell the difference between those who rarely get it right and those who generally get it right. We should always question what we read and what we see on TV.

Remember, people who write for newspapers, magazines, websites, or put stories on TV, are human and their business demands speed (particularly TV), which can sacrifice accuracy. That often leads to mistakes and bad information. The same First Amendment that protects respected news organizations like the New York Times and the Wall Street Journal also protects hate speech that has found a wide audience on the Internet.

We have laws for "libel" (written) and "slander" (verbal) that prevent people from writing or saying things they know are wrong, but write or say them anyway just to hurt someone. There is a very high standard for finding a news organization or an individual guilty of libel or slander. To successfully prove that libel or slander has occurred, you have to show that a news organization (libel) or a person (slander) maliciously planned to say something untrue that hurt you. So, libel or slander cases are rarely brought to court. It is even rarer for a court to find that those charges are true.

Speech that affects the safety of the general public is not allowed. For instance, people cannot yell "fire" in a crowded theater . . . or "shark" on a crowded beach . . . or "bomb" at your school. In these examples, the freedom of one person's speech must be measured against the safety of people who would be hurt in the panic that was caused to get out of the building or the water.

Similarly, while people are allowed to assemble freely, they cannot assemble in the middle of a busy highway. That presents a danger to the public health—as well as an interruption of the public transportation system and commerce. The freedom to assemble means people can gather to express ideas or join together in a common purpose—it doesn't mean small groups of people can affect what the rest of us do.

If a million people asked Congress to change something, or do something that Congress didn't want to do, Congress cannot make them stop asking. But if enough people agree about changing something, and Congress won't do what the people ask, members of Congress can risk losing their elections for office.

Second (II) Amendment
Gun Ownership as Foundation for Militias

When the U.S. was formed, the founders were very concerned about the possibility of another war. Citizen soldiers played a key role in the American Revolution, and to be ready for another war, the Founders wanted to make sure we could always preserve a citizen militia.

Congress made laws to regulate guns, and began to do that in the early part of the twentieth century to keep really dangerous guns away from criminals and the public-at-large, but these laws are always really unpopular. At the same time, there exists a constitutional right to own a gun. The Founders included the Second Amendment to keep a ready militia (or armed National Guard) throughout the states in case we needed to go to war quickly and the citizens needed guns to be prepared for a militia (or armed National Guard).

(The word "militias" here does NOT mean the anti-government radicals who became visible in the 1990s. In 1939, the Supreme Court said Congress could make laws restricting gun ownership, and said the Second Amendment's "obvious purpose" was to preserve an armed National Guard. In 2008, the Court said there is an individual right to have guns for self-defense and hunting, but still said the government can regulate gun rights.)

Third (III) Amendment
Housing of Soldiers

Soldiers have not been quartered (able to live) in civilian homes since the Constitution. But before that, the British soldiers stayed in peoples' homes when they were in charge. Also, during the American Revolution, British soldiers stayed in peoples' homes; that was one of the reasons the Founders included this amendment in our Bill of Rights.

During the Civil War, U.S. troops in the South often took over peoples' homes to use or stay in—but remember the southern states were in rebellion, so the army treated them as if they were no longer part of the U.S.

Fourth (IV) Amendment
Privacy Rights for Property and People

This is the amendment that makes it illegal for the government to take away personal property. People are safe from arrest, and their possessions and their information are safe from seizure by the police or the government, unless the police have a warrant from a judge.

Fifth (V) Amendment
Rights of Individuals in Criminal Cases

Rights under the Fifth Amendment include:

- Criminal charges must be brought by a grand jury;

- People don't have to testify against themselves;

- No one can take away a citizen's life, liberty, or property without applying the law; and,

- Private property cannot be taken for public use without a fair payment.

Once someone is tried for a crime, the Constitution say he or she cannot be tried for the same crime again. No matter what other evidence is found, even if the accused admits guilt (that he or she really did commit the crime), if they have already been tried for that crime and found innocent, they cannot be tried again.

To "Take the Fifth" means when someone is arrested, or while on trial, that person does not have to tell the police or the courts anything about what happened. That person does not have to explain himself or herself to anyone.

Sixth (VI) Amendment
Rights for a Fair Trial

This Amendment is the basis for our belief that people are "innocent until proven guilty" when they are tried in our courts and system of courts. Criminal protections in the Constitution for citizens include:

- A speedy, public trial and a fair jury in the place where the crime was committed;

- The accused must be advised of the charges and be able to face the witnesses against him or her;

- The accused is allowed to bring his or her own witnesses into the court-room; and,

- The accused gets to have the assistance of a lawyer for his defense.

Seventh (VII) Amendment
Rights in Civil Cases

The Founders thought a trial by jury was real important to a democracy. They made sure in the Sixth Amendment that people had a jury for criminal trials; and, the Seventh Amendment makes sure they have one for civil trials when the amount is in excess of twenty dollars in federal court. There are two kinds of civil punishments: money or an injunction (an injunction is an order to make somebody do something, or stop doing something). Since twenty dollars means something entirely different today than it did when the Constitution was written, nearly all civil trials have a jury now.

The difference between criminal trials and civil trials is this: criminal trials are held for crimes people commit against each other like stealing, killing, or physically hurting someone. Civil trials concern property. For instance, if two people think a farm is theirs, they go to court. The matter will be decided in a civil trial.

Eighth (VIII) Amendment
Bails, Fines, Punishments

Fines and bail are not generally decided based on someone's ability to pay. "Reasonable" means what most people could afford if they needed to pay for bail or a fine. "Reasonable" nearly always means that the fine or bail amount must be in proportion to the crime. If a judge says somebody is a "flight risk," bail could be very high. The judge does not have to allow bail if it seems like the accused could run away before the trial takes place.

Punishment under the Constitution cannot be "cruel and unusual." Over time, it is society that decides which punishments are cruel and unusual. We used to hang people in public for many crimes. Now, we reserve killing people for only the most horrible crimes, and we give people chances to appeal whatever punishment they are given by a judge. People still disagree about whether killing someone, for whatever crime they commit, is "cruel and unusual."

Ninth (IX) Amendment
Rights Retained By the People

The Constitution says that the rights it names cannot deny or abuse other rights of the people. The Founders worried that what they had written might be twisted and used against people because no matter how well-intentioned the ideals of anything are, they knew they could not dictate decency to people. They also knew that many people worried about losing some rights not listed in this new Constitution that existed before they came to this country from England. These were called "common" laws.

The Founders also believed people had certain rights granted by God. These were called "natural" laws. They wanted to make sure everyone knew that just because they only listed some rights in the Bill of Rights, they weren't getting rid of the natural laws or common laws that were so important to many people when the country began.

Tenth (X) Amendment
Powers Kept by the States and the People

The Founders wanted to be real specific that the Constitution should protect rights, not interfere with them in some way. They wanted to express their support for the states by saying the states can make any law not forbidden by the Constitution. Some people were worried that under the Constitution, the states would have little power, so they included this amendment. It is a catch-all amendment, giving any powers not otherwise noted in the Constitution to the states and to the people individually.

Eleventh (XI) Amendment
Lawsuits Against States

This amendment keeps citizens of one state from suing another state in federal court. It came about when a man from one state sued another state over an inheritance. When the Supreme Court decided that states could be sued, this amendment was passed to clarify the legal powers of the Supreme Court. People can still sue state officials in federal court, so the effect is not that great.

Twelfth (XII) Amendment
Election of the President and Vice President

Note: There is also a federal law that goes into more detail about how electing a President and Vice President works. This only covers what is in the Constitution.

An elector is one of several people responsible for casting his or her state's electoral votes for the candidates for President and Vice President who won the popular vote in the state. (Maine and Nebraska are the only two states that do not follow the "winner-take-all" rule that other states use. These two states cast their electoral votes proportionately [based on the popular vote for their state] to the candidates running for President.) State legislatures make rules to select electors, but they are nominated by their party. They are loyal to the people in the party they represent. Electors from each state are based on population; each state has a number of electors that equals the number of representatives and senators for that state.

When electors meet to elect the President and Vice President, they are generally called the Electoral College. The process begins when they go to a place in their states, write down their choice for President and for Vice President. Then they make a list of their selections for both offices, and the number of votes for each candidate. The electors sign and approve the list, seal the list and send it to Washington, D.C. Then, the Electoral College ceases to exist for another four years.

The President of the Senate (also the Vice President of the country, whose service will have just been completed) opens the votes before members of the House of Representatives and the Senate (whose service will have just started) and counts all the votes. The person who has a majority of Electoral votes will be the President. (Right now, there are a total of five hundred thirty-eight Electoral College votes; it takes two hundred seventy votes to have a majority.)

If nobody gets a majority, the House of Representatives picks the President, by ballot, from the presidential candidates who got the most electoral votes. If it happens this way, each <u>state</u> has a vote, so (currently) there will be no more than fifty votes.

The delegation of each state will determine how their states will vote. At least two-thirds of representatives in each state delegation must participate in the decision for how their state will cast a vote in this "contingent election." A majority of states (fifty percent plus one) of all the states (currently that would be twenty-six states) will be required to make this decision.

If there is not a decision before January 20 (the day the next President is supposed to take the oath of office), the Speaker of the House will serve as President.

The Senate picks the Vice President in the same fashion as the House of Representatives picks the President.

In 1801 (before the Twelfth Amendment), Thomas Jefferson was elected by the House of Representatives; in 1825 (after the Twelfth Amendment), Andrew Jackson was selected by the House; and in 1837 (also after the Twelfth Amendment), Martin Van Buren's Vice President, Richard Mentor Johnson, was selected by the Senate.

People continue to wonder why we don't just vote for a presidential ticket directly. The Electoral College has worked relatively well for more than two hundred years, with the notable exceptions of the 1801, 1825, 1837, 1876, 1888 and 2000 elections. Congress has tried several times to consider bills to eliminate the Electoral College, but none have gone very far.

Over the years, the Electoral College has evolved into a tradition that conveys legitimacy upon an elected candidate. It began as an institution to include the states in the election of the President and Vice President, and ease the fears of our Founders who worried that the general population was not quite smart enough to directly elect the President.

Some people think that the Electoral College protects the interests of smaller states since their populations are so small. However, presidential candidates who seek votes to win an election will always be drawn to states where they can get the most votes: a state with a larger number of Electoral votes (if we keep the Electoral College), or a state with a large population (if we get rid of the Electoral College).

So, the argument that small states, with their small populations, have more influence under the Electoral College system is mathematically flawed. Remember, electoral votes are based on population, so either way, large states will always be courted by candidates as the most important states, and the most needed by candidates to win an election . . . either with the Electoral College or without it.

It is possible for a person who won the most popular votes in an election, to lose the vote in the Electoral College. The most recent example of that happening is the 2000 election. Democrat Al Gore won the popular vote by more than 500,000 votes in the election, but lost the Electoral College by five votes.

Before the election of 2000, in 1824 John Quincy Adams won the Electoral College by fifteen votes, although Andrew Jackson won the popular vote by 37,237 votes (both men were in the same political party); in 1876, Republican Rutherford B. Hayes won the Electoral College vote by one vote, although Democrat Samuel J. Tilden won the election by 251,746 votes; in 1888, Republican Benjamin Harrison won the Electoral College vote by sixty-five votes, although Democrat Grover Cleveland won the election by 95,096 votes.

Thirteenth (XIII) Amendment
Abolishment of Slavery

The South maintained that the Civil War was over "states rights," a principle that says states can choose their own practices. But the thing the South wanted most to do differently from the North was to have slaves, so calling it "states rights" was just their way of disguising the issue. While we clearly fought the Civil War over the institution of slavery, the South did not agree with that prospect, and would continue to hide behind the fantasy of "states rights" while treating some voters unfairly well into the twentieth century.

After a bloody Civil War, those in Congress, and in the states, never wanted the question to be in doubt again—ever.

Fourteenth (XIV) Amendment
Equal Protection Under the Law for Everyone

The most fundamental principle this amendment put into the Constitution was the concept of equal protection under the law for every person living in the United States. It also emphasizes that anyone born in the United States is a citizen, entitled to the liberties of our citizens.

Not everyone who lived here when the Fourteenth Amendment was ratified was considered a citizen with all the protections the Constitution offered our citizens. Slaves were never considered full people (they would not have been counted at all, but for purposes of maximizing the population in Southern states), much less citizens whose liberties were protected by the Constitution.

The Fourteenth Amendment was clear that if states did not want to let some people vote, like former slaves or their children, the congressional representation for that state was to be reduced. However, nearly all the Southern states found ways to limit the voting freedoms of black citizens, and their representation was never decreased. The shadow of slavery, and how we reacted to it, haunts us still. Today, we still must work at protecting the rights of every citizen.

The Fourteenth Amendment specifically denies giving any money to slave owners who lost slaves for any reason. It also did not allow a state or the government to pay any bills (payment) the South owed from their war against the U.S. But it did make sure that money for pensions or the debts of the people who fought to save the Union, got paid.

Fifteenth (XV) Amendment
Voting Rights

Slavery has been such a red-hot issue since the beginning of our nation. In fact, the Founders fought mightily over the institution of slavery as they wrote the Constitution with some Founders calling slavery the weak spot in our democracy and our Constitution. History proved them right; and, the Civil War very nearly killed the United States as it existed at that time. Slavery, disguised as "states rights," was at the core of the war. So, Congress felt strongly that people who were once slaves, or whose ancestors were slaves, needed constitutional protection for their right to vote.

Sixteenth (XVI) Amendment
Congress' Power to Tax

The question of taxes has always split the population between those with higher incomes and those with lower incomes. There's an old saying, "Where you stand depends on where you sit." People who pay more taxes generally feel like the system is less fair.

As the United States found the need to repay debts and wage the Civil War, Congress passed bills to create income taxes (taxes on money people earn). The Supreme Court first found those laws constitutional (during the Civil War), then later found a similar law unconstitutional. Since the nation's economic foundation was at stake, they passed the Sixteenth Amendment.

Seventeenth (XVII) Amendment
Direct Election of U.S. Senators

It took a long time for us to actually vote for our senators. The Constitution is very hard to change. But as the population became more aware of who served them in the Senate, and how they were chosen, it just became the right thing to do. Each state gets two senators; they serve six years and get one vote each. If a senator dies while in office, or leaves office for some reason, the governor of that state can appoint a temporary senator until a new election is held.

Eighteenth (XVIII) Amendment
Prohibition of Alcohol

Alcohol-related deaths and crime were considered a problem, perhaps even a larger problem than today, when this amendment was ratified. This amendment made it illegal (wrong) for citizens to make, sell, or transport (move to another place or state) any kind of drinking alcohol in or out of the United States. This is the only amendment ever invalidated (see the Twenty-First Amendment).

Nineteenth (XIX) Amendment
Women Get the Right to Vote

Misconceptions about what women can do were even worse when the country was founded. Women generally were not allowed to own property, vote, or participate in government. Even the thought of women voting upset the traditional power structure, and it was very scary to most men. Men who owned property did vote, and effectively controlled who could participate in our democracy. They did not think women were equal to them, or as smart as men. This amendment said it didn't matter if you were a man or a woman, as a United States citizen, you had the right to vote. Nobody ever wants to give up power.

Twentieth (XX) Amendment
Terms of Service for the President,
Vice President and Congress

Our elections are held in November; the following January, the President, Vice President and Congress take office. The term of office for the incoming President and Vice President begins at noon on January 20 of the year following their election. The term of service for the outgoing President and Vice President end at that same moment.

Terms of new senators and representatives begin at noon on January 3 of the year following their election. Terms of the former senators and representatives officially end at the same moment.

Congress must meet at least once every year (on January 3), unless they pass a law to pick another day (which they usually do if January 3 falls on a weekend).

If the new President (called President-Elect) dies after he gets elected, but before January 20, the new Vice President (called Vice President-Elect) will become President. If, for some reason, a President is not chosen before January 20, or if the President-Elect does not meet the rules set out in the Constitution, then the Vice President-Elect will act as President until someone is chosen as President.

If neither the President-Elect nor the Vice President-Elect meets the rules set out in the Constitution, the Congress can decide by law who will act as President, and how a President should then be picked. That person will act as President until the constitutional rules can be followed.

Congress can make a law to deal with other situations that might happen.

Twenty-First (XXI) Amendment
Repeal of Eighteenth (XVIII) Amendment

Prohibiting alcohol came to be seen as a violation of personal liberties. Police began to ignore citizens' civil rights in their efforts to find alcohol, or alcohol-related equipment. Also, many local governments and the federal government saw alcohol as a source of revenue (money), so the movement grew to get rid of this amendment. Plus, the Eighteenth Amendment actually increased crime. People didn't want to do without alcohol, so they turned to criminals called "bootleggers" to get it for them. The period of time when alcohol was forbidden was called "prohibition."

Alcohol remains the only drug made legal under the Constitution. Tobacco is legal, but by law, or statute, not through the Constitution.

Twenty-Second (XXII) Amendment
Limit of Presidential Terms

When the Congress passed this amendment, there was a very popular President from one political party, and the majority in Congress was from the other major party. The Congress was sure presidential terms should be limited. Eventually, most people began to agree that eight years was long enough for a President to carry out his or her programs and long enough for one person to serve in the highest office in the land.

A President may serve only two, four-year terms. If someone has been President, or acted as President for more than two years of another President's term, they can only be elected once more.

Twenty-Third (XXIII) Amendment
Washington, D.C., Electors for President

Washington, D.C., gets the same number of presidential electors (three) as do the smallest states. They meet as electors in the District of Columbia and follow the rules of the Twelfth Amendment.

Washington, D.C., doesn't have any senators and has only one representative in the House of Representatives, but this representative cannot vote. There are far-flung U.S. territories that are in the same position, but they do not have electoral votes. Washington, D.C., is the only large population in the United States not fairly represented in Congress.

Since the 1970s, there has been a movement to make Washington, D.C., a state, but that would add two senators and at least one representative to the makeup of Congress. This would upset the balance of power, and nobody likes to lose power.

People in Washington, D.C., pay taxes like everybody else. The people who live there serve their country in war; and, they pay taxes just like citizens in any other state. They may eventually be added as a state, but that is for Congress to decide.

Twenty-Fourth (XXIV) Amendment
Elimination of the Poll Tax

In the early days of the United States in many states, only male property-owners could vote. The poll tax was used in these early days as a way to let non-property-owning males over twenty-one vote. It came to be (in the United States) a tax people paid to vote.

After the Civil War, the poll tax pretty much disappeared. But it came back in the 1890s and in the early 1900s as a way to promote white supremacy (a failed movement that promoted white people's superiority to everyone else). Voter registrars in the South were very crafty in the way that they applied the poll tax on African Americans. In some cases, they made the tax retroactive back to a person's twenty-first birthday, making the tax all the more difficult to pay.

Most states had already eliminated it when the Twenty-fourth Amendment passed. Only a few southern states still had it but it was used to keep poor people, usually African Americans, from voting. The South generally did all it could, for as long as it could, to keep African Americans from voting. It took several constitutional amendments to ensure that the basic rights of citizenship were available to everyone entitled to those rights under our Constitution.

Twenty-Fifth (XXV) Amendment
Succession of Office

If the President dies, leaves office or gets impeached, the Vice President becomes the President.

If there is not a Vice President, for whatever reason—if they die or something—the President will pick one and that person will be the Vice President after a majority of senators and representatives agree with the choice.

If the President gets shot or hurt or something happens to him or her, the President writes to the President of the Senate and the Speaker of the House of Representatives and tells them he or she can no longer do the job. The Vice President then becomes the Acting President. In order for the President who gave up the office (from being hurt or whatever) to get his or her job back, he or she has to write to the President of the Senate and the Speaker of the House again to let them know he or she can do the job again.

The President is not the only one who can say that he or she is not able to do the job. It's never been done before, but if the Vice President and a majority of the Cabinet officers write the President of the Senate and the Speaker of the House and tell them they think the President cannot do his or her job, the Vice President immediately becomes President.

If this happens, when the original President thinks he or she can do the job again, he or she must write to the President of the Senate and the Speaker of the House and tell them he or she can now do the job. Once this is done, the President will again have the powers of office—unless the Vice President and a majority of the Cabinet officers write the President of the Senate and the Speaker of the House within four days to tell them that is not the case. If all this happens, Congress will meet within forty-eight hours to decide the issue. Congress must act within twenty-one days of receiving the letter. If senators and representatives decide by a two-thirds vote that the original President cannot do the job, the Vice President continues to act as President. Otherwise, the President gets back his or her job back.

Twenty-Sixth (XXVI) Amendment
Right of Eighteen-Year-Old Citizens to Vote

This amendment was passed when there was a lot of controversy in this country about the Vietnam War. Eighteen-year-old men were being drafted in large numbers to fight in Southeast Asia. It quickly became a popular idea that if someone was old enough to die for their country, he was old enough to make decisions by voting in elections. However, young voters are the least likely group of voters to exercise their right to vote.

Twenty-Seventh (XXVII) Amendment
Determination of Congressional Pay Raises

Congress has a specific process by which they give themselves raises. They can vote for a raise, but it will not be effective until the next Congress. So anyone who voted for a raise for themselves will have to face the voters and be re-elected before they actually get that raise.

During the 1980s, people were mad about government policies that led to deficit spending (spending money you don't have). Lots of people thought Congress spent the money of the United States very badly. Congress made it worse when they gave themselves pay raises, which they did to attract the best and the brightest to serve in the government. But the average citizen saw it as Congress enriching itself at the nation's expense.

So they figured they needed a constitutional amendment to take care of it and this way seemed fair. Congress could still vote to give themselves a raise, but they would have to face the voters before it would take effect.

This amendment was actually part of the original Bill of Rights, but was not immediately ratified by the states. It took more than two-hundred years for this amendment to get the support of enough states to become part of the Constitution.

End of the Constitution as it now exists

Student Exercise in Democracy

If you had the chance to add to the United States Constitution now, or in the next few years, to improve our democracy, what would you want to add?

Since the Constitution is not finished, what are some other ideas for amendments to the Constitution? Debate them to understand why some things are just too hard to get agreement on by two-thirds of any group.

Remember, the Constitution has only been amended twenty-seven times in over two hundred years, so an amendment should be considered extremely necessary (very, very important) to make it part of the Constitution. Also, remember that the Founders gave Congress the ability to make laws to deal with anything they saw fit, so just about any issue people want to add to the Constitution can be dealt with by passing a law.

In every debate about a new amendment, the most important questions are: how important is this idea that it must be added to the Constitution, or can Congress or local governments just make a law, or a rule, to deal with this issue?

Assume your group has succeeded in convening a constitutional convention. Following are suggestions for amendments, along with a suggestion or two to consider as arguments for and against the various amendments. Don't limit anyone's imagination by only using these suggestions, or by sticking strictly to the way they are written.

If you can get two-thirds of any group to support an amendment, remember the actual process of adopting an amendment to the United States Constitution also requires that the amendment be adopted by two-thirds of the United States Congress and three-fourths of the states as well.

Incidentally, many of these amendments are actually proposed by someone in Congress, or the states, to amend the Constitution.

Fast Fact

After the Constitutional Convention, Benjamin Franklin was asked what kind of government they created. He said, "A republic, if you can keep it."

Proposed Amendments to the Constitution

PROPOSED AMENDMENT

The Balanced Budget Amendment

WHAT IT IS:

This amendment would require the government of the United States to balance its budget every single year from now on.

POINTS TO DISCUSS FOR THE AMENDMENT:

- The United States should never spend more money than it takes in; that just makes good sense.

- Families have to balance their own budgets, so why can't the government?

POINTS TO DISCUSS AGAINST THE AMENDMENT:

- What if the United States goes to war, or has a national emergency like a hurricane, or flood, or something that would require us to spend more money than we have right then to further the national cause, how should that be handled?

- Remember, most families have some sort of debt, either a mortgage on their house, a car note or some credit card bills. What do they do when they don't have enough money to pay their bills?

PROPOSED AMENDMENT

Protection of the United States flag

WHAT IT IS:

This amendment would make it illegal to burn the American flag, and anyone who did burn a U.S. flag would punished to the fullest extent of the law.

POINTS TO DISCUSS FOR THE AMENDMENT:

- The flag is the symbol of the country, and burning it diminishes the nation.

- People who burn the flag are traitors and deserve punishment for disrespecting the flag.

- Our flag flies over people who fight for our nation; burning it lessens their effort.

POINTS TO DISCUSS AGAINST THE AMENDMENT:

- The Constitution is the foundation of the country and the flag, while inspirational, is only a piece of cloth.

- The Constitution lays out a clear definition of what treason is: to aid and comfort enemies. Burning a flag doesn't comfort an enemy, more likely it would just confuse them.

- There is not currently a problem with lots of people burning flags. Why amend the Constitution to tend to a problem that doesn't exist?

PROPOSED AMENDMENT

Campaign Finance Reform

WHAT IT IS:

This amendment would limit the amount of money candidates could spend on their campaigns for office. In 2010, the Supreme Court found that all the laws Congress has passed – to control money that big businesses (corporations) give political campaigns – are unconstitutional. The Supreme Court said that the money of big businesses and moneyed interests is "speech" protected by the First Amendment. In this amendment Congress, along with the states, would get to decide what that limit is and how candidates can get money for campaigns.

POINTS TO DISCUSS FOR THE AMENDMENT:

- Far too much money is collected by candidates for federal office each year, largely from corporations and businesses—organizations that will be governed by the rules made by the Congress and the President.

- Democracy is hurt when money has more influence on elections than voters do.

- Money is a megaphone, not speech. Now corporations and their money hold an extraordinary place above ideas and individual citizens in elections.

POINTS TO DISCUSS AGAINST THE AMENDMENT:

- Everyone in our democracy, including companies and businesses, should be able to participate in elections, to whatever extent they choose.

- Businesses and corporations contribute to society more than individuals by paying more taxes and employing people.

PROPOSED AMENDMENT

Repeal the Sixteenth Amendment

WHAT IT IS:

This amendment would repeal the Sixteenth Amendment, allowing Congress to collect taxes based on population, or in another manner they choose (other than on the income of individuals or companies).

POINTS TO DISCUSS FOR THE AMENDMENT:

- Taxing people based on their incomes is unfair because someone who works harder to make more money shouldn't have to pay more taxes.

- Our Founders wanted the federal government to be very small. Taxing by income goes against that reasoning.

POINTS TO DISCUSS AGAINST THE AMENDMENT:

- Congress must raise money to do its job. Taxing citizens by income is the best way for Congress to get money to run the country, defend the nation and meet all of our financial obligations.

- Changing how we pay our bills would be enormously difficult to do. To support this amendment means deciding on a new way to pay our bills, totaling trillion of dollars annually.

PROPOSED AMENDMENT

The Victims' Rights Amendment

WHAT IT IS:

This amendment would give the victim of a crime, or the families of the victims of crimes, the right to be heard in the court during the trial of the accused person, and to be heard before the sentencing of a criminal.

POINTS TO DISCUSS FOR THE AMENDMENT:

- Criminals have too many protections given to them in the Bill of Rights, but the victims of crimes have no rights, and no say in what happens in the courtroom.

POINTS TO DISCUSS AGAINST THE AMENDMENT:

- Victims of crimes or their families are not on trial for their lives, or for any part of their lives. They don't need the rights or protections we give people accused of crimes.

PROPOSED AMENDMENT

Lowering Voting Age to Sixteen

WHAT IT IS:

This amendment would offer the right to vote to sixteen-year-old citizens.

POINTS TO DISCUSS FOR THE AMENDMENT:

- People mature earlier now. Sixteen-year-olds are better educated and should have the opportunity to vote for people who are making decisions on their behalf.

- Some sixteen-year-olds work and pay taxes.

POINTS TO DISCUSS AGAINST THE AMENDMENT:

- Most sixteen-year-olds are not mature enough to make decisions that affect our country. They haven't even finished high school yet. We should be very careful about how young our electorate is.

- The age of eighteen is generally the age of reason in our laws. The consent to marry, to make health-related decisions and to be drafted for war begins at age eighteen.

PROPOSED AMENDMENT

Prohibition of Tobacco

WHAT IT IS:

This amendment would make the growing, possession or selling of tobacco illegal in every U.S. state and territory.

POINTS TO DISCUSS FOR THE AMENDMENT:

- We abolished alcohol once, so this kind of amendment has been part of the Constitution before.

- Doctors have been telling us for years that tobacco is deadly; this is not just a bad habit, it is killing people, and costing us billions of dollars for healthcare.

POINTS TO DISCUSS AGAINST THE AMENDMENT:

- The best evidence against this amendment is the existence of the Twenty-First Amendment.

- Attempts to prohibit tobacco will only make it more expensive. Prohibiting it will also put tobacco farmers out of work, which will hurt our economy, and could put smokers in jail.

PROPOSED AMENDMENT

Prohibition of the Death Penalty

WHAT IT IS:

This amendment would no longer allow any criminal convicted in a state or federal court to be put to death for his or her crime, or crimes.

POINTS TO DISCUSS FOR THE AMENDMENT:

- The Bill of Rights says a punishment cannot be cruel or unusual; surely, killing someone is cruel and unusual

- In the ten most basic laws for Jews and Christians (the Ten Commandments), it is clearly stated that "Thou shalt not kill."

POINTS TO DISCUSS AGAINST THE AMENDMENT:

- The death penalty would keep criminals from ever committing a crime again, and show other criminals what could happen to them.

- The Bible also says, "An eye for an eye, a tooth for a tooth"; so, if we follow what that statement says, if somebody kills somebody, it is okay to kill them.

What other ideas do you have for proposed amendments to the Constitution?

Separating the Powers

Explore the role of each of the branches of government (Judicial, Legislative, Executive) in these instances by having different groups of people play the part, or parts, of the different branches.

Congress overwhelmingly passes a law that is not entirely constitutional.

- The President does not sign it; it does not become law.

—OR—

- The President signs it; it becomes law.

- The people who do not agree with the law file a case in the courts asking the Supreme Court to rule on whether the law is constitutional or unconstitutional.

- Lawyers for the President and the Congress file opinions with the Court.

- The Supreme Court finds the law constitutional.

—OR—

- The Supreme Court finds the law unconstitutional. (Then, Congress can pass another law following the Supreme Court's guidelines.)

—OR—

- The Supreme Court can strike down the part of the law that is unconstitutional and leave the rest of the law in place.

Congress passes a law the President does not like.

- The President can veto it (say no), and stop the bill from becoming law.

- The Congress can try to "override" the veto with two-thirds of representatives and two-thirds of senators voting to make the bill law, despite what the President thinks.

The President agrees to send military troops somewhere overseas without Congress' permission (this has never happened).

- Congress could not allow any money to be spent for these purposes.

- Someone could file suit in federal court claiming the Commander-in-Chief acted unconstitutionally.

- The Supreme Court would act on the constitutional questions arising from the President making a claim that commits the military to battle.

Congress impeaches the President.

- The House of Representatives passes "articles of impeachment" against the President.

- The Senate acts as a jury and hears the case as if they were in a courtroom, listening to arguments between the lawyers for the President, and lawyers accusing the President.

- The Supreme Court's Chief Justice would sit in judgment during the Senate trial.

- The Senate votes to find the President not guilty.

—OR—

- The Senate votes to find the President guilty.

- The Vice President would prepare to serve as President, appointing (for the Senate to approve) a new Vice President.

The President suddenly dies while in office.

- The Vice President finds the Attorney General, or Justice of the Supreme Court (or another judge), to administer the constitutional oath of office.

- The new President appoints a new Vice President, submitting his or her name to the Senate for approval.

- The Supreme Court answers any questions about the transfer of power.

**The President is badly hurt and cannot continue
to serve as President.**

- The President (or Cabinet) writes to the President of the Senate and the Speaker of the House of Representatives telling them he or she can no longer do the job and that the Vice President will become Acting President.

- When the originally-elected President feels she or he could do the job again, he or she writes to the President of the Senate and the Speaker of the House of Representatives, telling them he or she is ready to resume the job and relieves the Acting President of his or her duties.

- The Supreme Court hears from anyone who is unhappy with any manipulation (sneaky handling) of the constitutional process.

**The Vice President and a majority of the President's advisors
(Cabinet) believe the President should no longer be serving
as President.**

- The Vice President and a majority of the President's advisors (Cabinet) write to the President of the Senate and the Speaker of the House of Representatives telling them the President of the United States can no longer do the job and that the Vice President will become Acting President.

- When the originally-elected President feels he or she can do the job again, or if the originally-elected President disagrees with the Vice President and Cabinet about his or her ability to perform the job of President, the originally-elected President writes to the President of the Senate and the Speaker of the House of Representatives, telling them he or she is resuming the job and relieving the Acting President of his or her duties.

- But if the original Vice President and a majority of the President's advisors (Cabinet) write to the President of the Senate and the Speaker of the House of Representatives within four days telling them they disagree that the originally-elected President is able to resume office, then Congress must meet within forty-eight hours and decide the matter twenty-one days after receiving the letter.

- The House of Representatives and the Senate must decide who serves as President with a vote of two-thirds of their members.

- The Supreme Court hears from someone who is unhappy with any manipulation of the constitutional process.

No presidential candidate wins a majority of electoral votes.

- The House of Representatives chooses the President by ballot in this manner: each state casts one vote; the members of the House of Representatives from each state meet to decide within their state delegations how their state vote will be cast in the "contingent election."

- To take the vote, the House needs at least one House member from at least two-thirds of the states.

- A majority of those states (fifty percent plus one) voting determine the next President of the United States.

- At the same time, the Senate chooses the next Vice President from the two candidates with the most electoral votes.

- At least two-thirds of senators must vote on this choice, and a majority (fifty percent plus one) makes the final choice for Vice President.

- The Supreme Court hears from anyone who is unhappy with any manipulation of the constitutional process.

The Math of a Presidential Campaign

Since we now have a better idea of how presidential candidates get elected, see which states you think are the most important to visit in order to get the two hundred seventy electoral votes needed to win a presidential election.

Here are the number of votes each state has in the Electoral College until 2020:

Alabama, 9	Kentucky, 8	North Dakota, 3
Alaska, 3	Louisiana, 8	Ohio, 18
Arizona, 11	Maine, 4	Oklahoma, 7
Arkansas, 6	Maryland, 10	Oregon, 7
California, 55	Massachusetts, 11	Pennsylvania, 20
Colorado, 9	Michigan, 16	Rhode Island, 4
Connecticut, 7	Minnesota, 10	South Carolina, 9
Delaware, 3	Mississippi, 6	South Dakota, 3
District of Columbia, 3	Missouri, 10	Tennessee, 11
Florida, 29	Montana, 3	Texas, 38
Georgia, 16	Nebraska, 5	Utah, 6
Hawaii, 4	Nevada, 6	Vermont, 3
Idaho, 4	New Hampshire, 4	Virginia, 13
Illinois, 20	New Jersey, 14	Washington, 12
Indiana, 11	New Mexico, 5	West Virginia, 5
Iowa, 6	New York, 29	Wisconsin, 10
Kansas, 6	North Carolina, 15	Wyoming, 3

The eleven most populous states (the states who have the most people living in them) in the country (California, Florida, Georgia, Illinois, Michigan, New Jersey, New York, North Carolina, Ohio, Pennsylvania and Texas) control how many electoral votes?

The next group of states, those that have ten electoral votes or more (Arizona, Indiana, Maryland, Massachusetts, Minnesota, Missouri, Tennessee, Virginia, Washington and Wisconsin), control how many electoral votes?

The remaining twenty-nine states, each having less than ten electoral votes apiece, control how many electoral votes among them?

Some of the top ten or eleven states are usually loyal to one political party or the other, so candidates mark those accordingly, then decide on a strategy of putting together a majority of two hundred seventy electoral votes from the states on the next tier of electoral states (those with at least ten votes) or some of the other twenty-nine states.

How many electoral votes does your state have?

If you were working for a presidential campaign, or if you were running for President, which states would you try the hardest to win to get the two hundred seventy votes needed to win the Electoral College?

Do you think the Electoral College is still a good way to elect a President? Or should we elect a President like we elect representatives, senators and other people who serve in public office (through direct elections, whoever gets the most votes wins)?

What are the chances we would elect a President through direct elections, whoever gets the most votes wins?

What Constitutional Privilege Do These Things Violate?

Choose which individual liberties, guaranteed by the Bill of Rights, the following actions would violate. (Some may violate none at all.)

- Somebody stands across the street from the police station, not interrupting anybody's work. This person gives a speech for the whole day about how the police are using tactics that are illegal, and the person making the speech gets arrested.

- Somebody gets arrested, but the police don't tell him or her the reason for the arrest.

- People sent a petition to Congress asking them to fix something, and Congress doesn't do it.

- Congress passes a law forbidding a "Keepers of the Faith" religion (or they pass a law that prohibits ANY religion).

- Army commanders require area homeowners to let soldiers stay in their homes when there is a housing shortage.

- Congress passes a law saying people can't pray in public.

- Congress passes a law keeping people from buying a certain kind of gun.

- A judge makes a person on trial tell why they broke the law.

- The government shuts down a newspaper because they wrote something that was really wrong about something, or someone, important (but they didn't mean to, they were just bad at their job).

- The Ku Klux Klan is denied a permit to gather in a town to stage a peaceful protest.

Bibliography

The Constitution of the United States. Commission on the Bicentennial of the United States Constitution, Eighteen Edition (with 27th Amendment), Washington, D.C., Government Printing Office: 1992.

The Constitution of the United States of American As Amended, H. Doc. No. 102-188, United States House of Representatives, 102nd Congress, 2nd Session, Washington, D.C., Government Printing Office: 1992.

The Constitution of the United States, Analysis and Interpretation, 1996 Supplement. Congressional Research Service, Washington, D.C., Government Printing Office: 1997.

Report to Accompany S.J. Res. 14, 72nd Congress, 1st Session. United States Senate Committee on the Judiciary, Washington, D.C., Government Printing Office: 1932.

Dellinger, W. "The Legitimacy of Constitutional Change: Rethinking the Amendment Process," *Harvard Law Review.* Boston, MA, Harvard University Press: 1993.

FindLaw International Legal Resources. http://supreme.lp.findlaw.com

Peirce, N. and Longley, L.D. *The People's President*. New Haven, CT, Yale University Press: 1981.

Simendinger, A., Barnes, J.A., and Cannon, C.M. "After the Great Close Call," *National Journal.* Washington, D.C., National Journal Group, Inc., November 18, 2000.

U.S. Electoral College: List of States and Votes: 2004, Allocation of Electoral Votes based on the 2000 Census. National Archives and Records Administration, Federal Register.http://www.archives.gov/federal_register/electoral_college/2004_certificates/index.html

Venetoulis, T.G. *The House Shall Choose*. Margate, NJ, Elias Press: 1968.

Special thanks to the following:

Dr. Sylvia Golombek, PhD

Ms. Nancy Bacot

Mr. Peter Smith, Esquire

Mr. Bert Peña, Esquire

Mr. Lawrence L. Calvert, Jr., Esquire

Ms. Darlene DenHollander, Esquire

Ms. Clara Pizaña

Mr. Chris Robicheaux

Mr. Bill Miles

Ms. Gail Bomer

Ms. Sandra Winslow

Other books by Cathy Travis:

REMEMBER WHO YOU ARE (a novel): From a Capitol Hill confirmation hearing, Judge Jodie Davis – a nominee to the U.S. Supreme Court – tells the U.S. Senate about her childhood in northeast Arkansas in the turbulent South of the late civil rights era. The lives of young Jodie's neighbors are thrown into turmoil – first when a black family tries to buy a house in their neighborhood, then by a monster tornado roiling through their town. But none of that prepares them for the chaos in the aftermath of a murder on the football field of the high school. The decisions that everyone makes in the aftermath have enormous consequences for each one of them.

ELECTED (a novel): Inaugurated after a bitter recount in Florida following the 2000 presidential race, President Hal Cord leads an angry and divided nation. **ELECTED** follows the Cord administration through the race to prevent al Qaeda attacks, and their success and mistakes on the international and domestic fronts. White House Press secretary MJ Bennett watches in horror as her country is brutally attacked, and careens into a Central Asian war that threatens the life of her new love, a legendary Special Forces commander.
After September 11, 2001, Cord calls for a creative "worldwide war." Sending an overwhelming military force to Afghanistan badly damages Osama bin Laden's force there; and Cord's focus on eliminating the combustible engine forces al Qaeda to morph quicker than the group had planned, with dangerous results for Saudi Arabia … and the United States.

TARGET SITTING is a heartbreakingly candid journal written when Travis was a Capitol Hill staffer. Beginning the week after the September 11, 2001 attacks – **TARGET SITTING** carries readers through that heart-pounding day, the anthrax attack on the Hill, and the full body shudder associated with working at the seat of government in the ensuing years. **TARGET SITTING** is a stark look at life in the target that al Qaeda missed in 2001.

For direct links to the books, go to <u>www.travisbooks.com</u>

Made in the USA
Lexington, KY
13 December 2016